The COMPACT &
DIGITAL
CAMERA
HANDBOOK

The COMPACT & DIGITAL CAMERA HANDBOOK

Successful photography with the new generation of cameras

DANIEL LEZANO

MARSHALL PUBLISHING • LONDON

A Marshall Edition
Conceived, edited and designed by
Marshall Editions Ltd
The Orangery
161 New Bond Street
London W1Y 9PA

First published in the UK in 1999 by Marshall Publishing Ltd

ISBN 1 84028 258 4

Originated in Singapore by HBM Print
Printed and bound in Italy by New Interlitho Spa

Project editor Jane Chapman
Art editor Phil Gamble
Managing editor Clare Currie
Managing art editor Helen Spencer
Editorial director Ellen Dupont
Art director Dave Goodman
Production Nikki Ingram, James Bann
DTP editor Lesley Gilbert
Editorial coordinator Becca Clunes

Contents

Introduction   6

Cameras and equipment   8
The main types of compact   10
The 35mm compact camera   14
The Advanced Photo System   22
The digital camera   28
Lenses   36
Focusing systems   42
Exposure   48
Film   56
Buying a camera   64
Care and maintenance   68
Film processing   70
Accessories   72

Techniques   76
Composition   78
Contrasting colours   86
Landscapes   90
People   100
Still life   110
Close-ups   116
Black-and-white documentary   120
Travel   126
Animals   132
Architecture   138
Stained-glass windows   144
Night scenes   148
Sunsets   156
Silhouettes   164
Patterns   168
Special effects   174

Digital imaging   184
Hardware   186
Peripherals   190
Software   198
Digital darkroom   202

Troubleshooting   204
Self-test   208
Glossary   212
Stockists   218
Index   220
Acknowledgments   224

Introduction

This book has been written for the huge (and growing) number of compact and digital camera users. With essential advice on the latest technology, this handbook will show you how you can use the new cameras to take great pictures.

I don't know anyone with so many photographs as my parents. They have recorded every stage of our family life in picture form, including my life, from baby to toddler to teenager and beyond. No doubt the same can be said for parents all around the world.

Since I was surrounded by cameras from an early age, it's no surprise that I, too, caught the bug. I've taken photos for as long as I can remember and, like most people, a compact was the first type of camera I used. It was a very basic instamatic, sporting a noisy film wind-on crank and flimsy plastic build – the sort of camera owned by hundreds of thousands of other people. The quality of the results was poor, but taking pictures with it was tremendous fun, and I haven't looked back since.

Technology has certainly changed since then. Compact cameras now offer advanced features such as autofocus, autoexposure, built-in flashguns and motorwinds, to name but a few. Amateur photographers have never had it so good!

The 1990s have been a particularly exciting time for photographers. Digital technology has finally become a viable method of creating images for the general user, as costs have fallen and image quality has improved considerably.

A computer is now standard in most schools, homes and offices. This means that everybody can try digital imaging – something that was unheard of not too long ago. Digital imaging equipment is now very easy to use, too.

Conventional film technology has not fallen by the wayside, however. Not only does film produce better colours and finer grain than ever before, there is now a major alternative to the standard 35mm format. The Advanced Photo System (APS), launched in 1996, promised to provide strong competition for 35mm film, and has not failed to impress.

So what does all this mean for the average snapshot photographer? To begin with, there is so much variety, with a camera to suit every occasion. Also, picture-taking has never been easier, thanks to the advanced automatic features that remove much of the fuss, but none of the enjoyment, of taking photographs. Cameras are also more versatile, with zoom lenses becoming increasingly popular, thanks to the flexibility and convenience they offer.

All this, and the fact that cameras are more affordable than ever, means that photography has never been so popular.

Covering all the major types of APS, 35mm compacts and digital cameras, this comprehensive, informative and easy-to-follow handbook will help you to develop your skills and guide you on your photographic journey.

The first chapter deals with the three main types of camera mentioned above and looks at their general features, including lenses, focusing and metering systems. There is also a comprehensive section dealing with film for compact cameras and buying advice for would-be camera purchasers.

The second chapter covers the use of the camera in photographing the most popular subjects, from landscapes and people to night scenes and special effects. Basic photographic principles are explained and there is advice on selecting the right camera, film and exposure for any given situation. Hundreds of inspirational photographs will show you what you can hope to achieve with a little practice, experience and creativity.

The third chapter takes a look at the hardware and software needed for digital imaging. As well as dealing with computer equipment, it looks at the best accessories ('peripherals') and software for getting the most out of digital imaging with compact and digital cameras.

There is a troubleshooting section to help you avoid some of the common pitfalls and a glossary to guide you through the technical jargon.

Try to complete the many projects aimed at developing your skills. You can find out exactly how much you have learned by attempting the self-tests at the back of the book.

I hope this book will inspire you to have fun with photography. Remember, the camera and the computer are only tools for expressing your own imagination and creativity. Who knows where they will take you!

Daniel Lezano

❂ Modern compact and digital cameras are packed with an amazing array of features. The Minolta Vectis 300 (below left) is a stylish zoom compact which uses the APS film format, while the Olympus Camedia C-900 (below right) is a digital camera capable of excellent results.

Chapter One

CAMERAS & EQUIPMENT

With so many different cameras on the market, choosing the one that is right for you can seem bewildering. Once you get past the first hurdle of deciding whether to go for a compact camera using 35mm or APS film, or a digital camera, you will then need to decide which features, such as zoom lenses and autofocus systems, will best suit your photographic needs. Packed with comprehensive but accessible information, this chapter will help you to make an informed choice so that you can get the most out of your camera. As well as reviewing the main features of compact and digital cameras, there is also essential advice on everything from exposure, focusing systems and red-eye reduction to choosing the right film and accessories.

The main types of compact

Although compact cameras are designed to be straightforward to use, there are many different models offering a variety of features. This section focuses on what is available, so you can decide which compact will best suit your photographic needs.

Fixed-lens compacts
Because these cameras feature a single lens of fixed focal length, they are among the smallest and thinnest on the market. In fact, some, such as the Ricoh GR1, are only a couple of millimetres thicker than a 35mm film cassette. The lens is usually wide-angle, ranging from 28mm to 38mm. This means that camera shake, which causes blurred pictures, is less likely to occur than with zoom compacts of longer focal length.

Most fixed-lens compacts are found at the budget end of the price range. However, there are some models which offer superb lens and build quality. The Olympus Mju II, for example, features a weatherproof body, a quality autofocus 35mm f/2.8 lens and spot metering.

Zoom compacts
These are by far the most popular type of compact camera. The zoom lens offers far more versatility and convenience than a

fixed-lens model. The extra 'pulling' power of a zoom lens means you are able to pull in distant subjects, making them appear closer than they really are.

The average zoom range is around 38–80mm, which is adequate for general picture-taking. Some models give more at the wide-angle end, making them more suitable for landscape photography. Others boast an extremely powerful telephoto zoom for pulling in very distant subjects, but these have limited range at the wide-angle end. These include models such as the Pentax Espio 200, with its incredible 48–200mm zoom. For portraits, look for a camera with a zoom

that includes 100mm in its range, as this is the ideal setting for this type of shot.

The only real drawback to these zoom compacts is that the maximum aperture at the telephoto end is relatively slow. This increases the risk of camera shake in all but bright conditions, unless a fast film is used.

Rangefinders

The term 'rangefinder' refers to the unique focusing system of this type of camera. With some models, the viewfinder features a rectangle with a 'ghost' image of the central part of the scene. To get a sharp image, you focus the lens until this 'registers' (or overlaps perfectly) with the main viewfinder image.

1: Fixed-lens compact
2-6: Zoom compacts
7: Rangefinder with interchangeable lens

There are not too many of these cameras on sale today and what there is can be found at the top end of the price range. Some rangefinders form part of a large photographic system, with interchangeable lenses and accessories, such as motordrives and flashguns.

Single-use cameras

Also known as disposables, these compacts come pre-loaded with film and are ready to use. Single-use cameras are very cheap and perfect for occasions, such as a night on the town, where there is a risk of losing a more expensive camera. Many different versions are available using 35mm or APS film. They are available with or without a built-in flash,

and with colour or black-and-white film, while some are designed for use underwater. Almost all feature a wide-angle lens, as this is the best type for general snapshots, although there is a model from Fuji which has a 100mm telephoto lens.

Image quality from single-use cameras may not be top quality, but they are an ideal choice for fun, fuss-free snaps.

Weather-resistant and waterproof cameras

Some fixed- and zoom-lens compacts are weather resistant, while others are designed for use underwater. Although these two terms are similar, they do not mean exactly the same thing.

1: Waterproof compact
2: Instant camera
3: Single-use camera

A weather-resistant camera is designed for use in all types of conditions and will not be damaged by heavy rain. However, the camera should not be submerged in water, as the outer casing is not completely watertight.

If you're looking for a compact to use underwater, then you need a model which is waterproof. These cameras usually feature a thick, bright-yellow exterior, and are capable of working up to depths of around five metres.

Instant cameras

If you want to see your pictures in a hurry, then nothing is quicker than an instant camera. These use an innovative film system that produces photographs within minutes.

Polaroid and Fuji both produce affordable instant cameras. Although image quality from both systems is reasonably good, the range of camera features is limited and the packs of film are quite expensive. ■

Other types of compact

Over the years a number of unusual compacts have come onto the market. Some never took off, others have stood the test of time.

Cartridge cameras

These budget cameras were designed with ease of use in mind by having the film stored in small cartridges. The two main types of cartridge, 110 and 127, use smaller films than the 35mm format, resulting in average quality.

Half-frame cameras

Keep an eye out in second-hand shops for cameras such as the Yashica Samurai. These compacts, known as half-frame cameras, use standard 35mm film, but record an image half the size of a normal shot. This means that twice as many photos can be recorded on a roll of film, but quality is sacrificed.

Novelty compacts

Novelty cameras are an excellent way to introduce children to photography. The basic fixed-focus lens isn't particularly good in terms of quality, but this isn't important. These cheap and cheerful compacts could be the first step in producing the next master photographer!

Disc system

Kodak introduced a radical new format in the 1980s known as the Disc system. It was based around a thin disc holding 15 frames, and wafer-thin cameras. Unfortunately, the cameras never caught on and they were later discontinued, although the film is still available through some outlets.

Minox spy cameras

These models are characterized by their small size and unusual 8x11 film. They are often called spy cameras, as they are easy to conceal and operate very quietly. However, purchasing film and processing can be a problem, making these cameras more suitable for the enthusiast than the average compact user.

The 35mm compact camera

Easy to use and boasting a range of sophisticated features, the 35mm compact is an enduringly popular model and is often the first camera people use. The most important features of this versatile camera are discussed below.

Many of the features, such as the integral flash and self-timer, are also found on Advanced Photo System (APS) and digital cameras, but to avoid repetition only 35mm compacts are covered in detail in this section.

THE MAIN FEATURES
Lens
There are two main types, the fixed lens and the zoom lens. The quality of the optics in the lens plays a major part in the sharpness of your pictures. Lenses are covered in more detail on pages 36–41.

Flash sensor and light sensor
These sensors help to produce the correct exposure by detecting the amount of light or reflected flash reaching the camera from the subject.

Infrared transceiver
This is used by the autofocus system to work out how far the subject is from the

FRONT VIEW

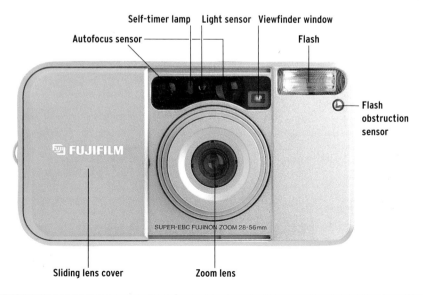

Self-timer lamp   Light sensor   Viewfinder window

Autofocus sensor

Flash

Flash obstruction sensor

FUJIFILM

SUPER-EBC FUJINON ZOOM 28-56mm

Sliding lens cover   Zoom lens

TOP VIEW

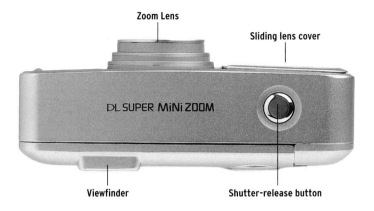

Zoom Lens

Sliding lens cover

DL SUPER MiNi ZOOM

Viewfinder

Shutter-release button

REAR VIEW

Viewfinder

LCD panel

Autofocus lamp

Multi-function button

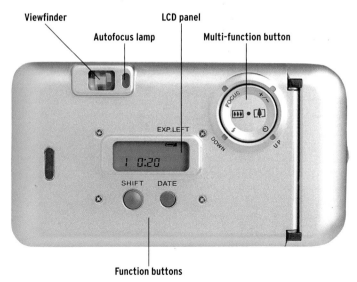

EXP.LEFT

SHIFT   DATE

Function buttons

Top tip

■ To check if your camera has DX-coding, open the back; if there are metal pins in the film chamber, then it does. Very cheap cameras and those made before DX-coding was introduced may need to have the film speed set manually.

camera. The transceiver sends out an infrared beam which is reflected back by the subject. The camera interprets this as a distance measurement.

Subject-biased exposure modes

In addition to the standard automatic mode, some cameras offer a choice of exposure modes suited to particular subjects. The camera makes slight adjustments to its aperture/shutter speed combination as well as to the flash and film transport systems.

PORTRAIT MODE The camera selects a wide aperture to throw the background out of focus and automatically switches on the flash to provide fill-in light and the red-eye reduction facility.

CLOSE-UP MODE The camera selects a smaller aperture to increase the depth-of-field and, if the camera has multi-point AF (see page 45), it uses the central focusing point for focusing and metering.

LANDSCAPE MODE A small aperture is selected for good depth-of-field and the automatic flash is switched off.

LCD

LCD is an abbreviation for Liquid Crystal Display. The LCD on most compacts provides plenty of information including the flash mode, battery condition and the frame counter. Most compacts have the LCD on the top or back of the camera, with all the main function buttons conveniently located around it.

Self-timer

This function sets a ten-second delay between the shutter button being pressed and the picture being taken. Use this facility when you want to be in the frame but there's no-one around to take the photo for you. Some cameras have a two-shot self-timer that takes a second picture shortly after the first.

Infinity mode

This sets the focusing to infinity and is useful for shooting through glass. Refer to the section on focusing systems on pages 42–47 for more details.

DX-coding

DX-coding was introduced by Kodak in 1983. It is a system that allows cameras and processing machines to automatically identify information about 35mm film.

DX-code markings are found on the cassette and take the form of a chequerboard pattern of rectangles. They are made up of two rows of silver (conductive) and black (insulated) rectangles that, when in contact with metal pins in the camera's film chamber, provide information on the film speed, latitude and number of exposures.

Motorwind

Most compacts feature a motorwind that automatically advances the film after each exposure and rewinds the film after the final frame has been taken. Some models boast a continuous mode that keeps taking photographs and advancing the film until the shutter button is released – which is an extremely useful feature for action photography.

Remote control

A remote-control facility allows you to fire the camera from a range of about five metres and provides an alternative to the self-timer.

Viewfinder

The viewfinder is the window through which you compose the picture, and is an easily overlooked feature. The size of the viewfinder varies from camera to camera and it's worth making sure you're happy with the size before you buy. Some cameras have very large viewfinders which provide very bright and clear images – ideal for composing a shot. Many cheaper models and several zoom compacts have smaller viewfinders which can be difficult to use, especially if you wear glasses. Common viewfinder features include:

TWIN LEDS These light emitting diodes are found on the side of the viewfinder and light up to provide information on the autofocus and flash systems. A green LED is the standard colour for the focusing system. It lights when the camera has focused correctly and flashes if the autofocus system is having problems. An orange or red LED indicates the status of the integral flash. The LED flashes while the flashgun recharges and stays lit when the flash is fully charged.

FRAME LINES/PARALLAX CORRECTION LINES The lines around the edge of the viewfinder give an approximate guide to the edge of the frame.

Many compact cameras also feature additional markings at the top of the frame, known as parallax correction lines. These are used to help you compose the picture accurately when shooting close-ups. You need these because the viewfinder is positioned above (and usually to the left) of the lens, giving a slightly different view than the lens. See the Close-ups section on pages 116–119 for more details.

DIOPTRIC ADJUSTMENT This handy facility is most commonly found on zoom compacts and allows spectacle wearers to adjust the sharpness of the viewfinder to suit their eyesight.

Film loading

To load a film, open the camera back and drop the film into the chamber. The film leader (the end of the film sticking out of the cassette) must be pulled until its tip reaches a marker on the camera body. Once the back is closed the film should wind on. With most compacts, if the film is not loaded correctly, an 'E' flashes on the LCD to warn you to try again. Some cameras wind the entire film out of the cassette after loading so that as you take pictures, the film is wound back into the cassette. This means that should the film back be opened while a film is loaded, only the unused part of the film is ruined.

Multiple exposures

If you're keen to try your hand at special effects, then this feature is worth having. Selecting multiple exposures disengages the motorwind and allows you to take two or more exposures on the same frame of film. Getting good results depends on experimentation and luck, but with practice, interesting results are possible. You can learn more about multiple exposures in the Special effects section on pages 182–183.

Backlighting compensation (BLC)

Taking a picture of someone with a bright background behind them is likely to result in the subject being underexposed and therefore appearing extremely dark in the photograph. The backlighting compensation facility exposes the film for longer and gives a better exposure on the subject.

Macro mode

This facility allows you to take a photograph to within about 30cm or closer of the subject, and is extremely useful if you want to take close-up pictures of flowers or small creatures.

Panoramic facility

Landscapes often include a lot of sky in the top third of the frame and lots of dull foreground in the bottom third. Switching to panoramic mode operates blinds inside the camera that prevent any light reaching the top and bottom third of the frame, so that only the central third is exposed. Don't be afraid to use the panoramic format in an upright position if the subject is tall and narrow.

Backlighting Compensation

These two shots show the effect of using the BLC facility. The shot on the left, taken with the camera in auto mode, shows a grossly underexposed subject. The second shot, taken from an identical position, uses the camera's BLC facility to increase the exposure and reveal much more detail on the subject.

⋂ Without BLC the shot is underexposed. ⋂ With BLC much more detail is visible.

Interval shooting

This is a clever feature that takes a series of pictures at regular intervals. It can be used to show how a scene changes over the course of a day, or to capture the stages of a flower opening.

Bulb mode

This function keeps the shutter open for as long as you want, and is worth experimenting with for interesting night or low-light photography. Some models offer a bulb with flash facility, a variation on the slow-synchronization mode (see opposite page). There is more on the Bulb mode in the Special effects section on pages 176–177.

Shutter speed range

The wider the range of shutter speeds on your camera, the more shooting situations it can cope with. A very fast shutter speed is necessary to freeze the action of fast-moving subjects, while slow shutter speeds allow for creative low-light and night-time photography.

Databack

On some cameras a databack comes as standard, on other models it is an optional facility. This function allows you to print the date or time in the bottom corner of the picture. Some models also allow captions, such as 'Happy Birthday' or 'Congratulations', to be imprinted on the photograph. This facility can be switched off when not required.

Batteries

The two most common types of batteries used in compacts are alkaline and lithium. Alkaline batteries are inexpensive and widely available. The two main sizes are AA and AAA.

Lithium batteries are becoming increasingly popular. Although they are more expensive than alkaline batteries, they last much longer and recharge the flash faster. The most common sizes are CR123A and CR2.

Slow-synchronization mode

These comparison pictures show the difference between using the flash in normal auto and slow-sync modes.

෴ This shot was taken in the normal auto mode and although the subject has been correctly exposed, the background is very dark.

෴ Setting the camera to slow-sync mode enables the subject to be correctly exposed while allowing the colourful decor in the background to be recorded. Remember that slow-sync flash requires the camera to be kept very steady to prevent camera shake.

Integral flashgun

A flashgun is a standard feature on all but the most basic compact cameras. The power of the flash varies from model to model, but is usually sufficient to illuminate a subject within a few metres of the camera. The flash system on compact cameras is very sophisticated to ensure correct exposure. The flash is balanced for daylight, which means that flash photographs give accurate reproduction without any colour casts.

The flash offers several modes to cater for different situations:

AUTOMATIC MODE This is the usual setting for the flash. The camera's exposure system measures the light level and fires the flash automatically if it decides it needs to.

FILL-IN FLASH MODE This function, which on some cameras is called forced-on or forced-flash, fires a low-power burst of light in bright conditions. It's a very useful facility when shooting portraits, as the flash removes shadows from the subject's face to produce a more pleasing result.

FORCED-OFF MODE The function of this mode is to prevent the flash from firing. You will rarely need to use this mode, unless you are in a venue where flash photography is not allowed, such as in an art gallery, church or museum. On these occasions, mount the camera on a tripod or any available flat surface, otherwise the slow shutter speed will result in camera shake.

SLOW-SYNCHRONIZATION MODE This very creative function, commonly called slow-sync or night-portrait mode, fires the flash and sets a long shutter speed. The flash exposes the main subject, while the relatively long exposure results in background details being recorded. The camera should be mounted on a tripod, although hand-holding it can produce some bizarre effects, in the form of streaks of light.

RED-EYE REDUCTION MODE The most common problem associated with using the flash is red eye. The reduction mode fires a series of flash bursts or a continuous beam of light before the main flash exposure in an attempt to reduce the problem. ■

Fill-in flash

These two portraits show how using fill-in flash can improve your portrait photography. The first, taken using only daylight, reveals quite a few shadows under the subject's eyes. For the second picture, fill-in flash was used, removing the shadows and producing a far brighter portrait. Another benefit of fill-in flash is the reflection of the flash in the eyes, known as catchlights, which adds a little extra sparkle to the result.

◗ Without fill-in flash   ◗ With fill-in flash

Red eye

This is caused by light reflecting back off the retina in the eye. It is common in the following instances:

1. In low light, when the pupils of the eyes are wide open.
2. In photographs of babies and children. The reaction in the muscles of their eyes to flash light is slower than in adults, so they are more at risk from red eye.
3. In pictures taken at parties or social events, because alcohol slows the reaction times of the subject's eyes.

Other factors that affect the chances of red eye in photographs include:

1. The type of camera. Red eye can be a problem with all types of compact camera but it is most common with zoom compacts. This is because the maximum aperture of the zoom is relatively small, so a strong flash output is required for the correct exposure.
2. The distance between the flash and the lens. The closer the flash is to the lens, the narrower the angle of the flash and the more likely the risk of red eye.

Compact cameras are getting smaller and smaller but one drawback of this is that the flash is nearer to the lens, thus increasing the risk of red eye, even if the red-eye reduction mode is activated.

Avoiding red eye

1. Make sure the camera's red-eye reduction mode is selected, if available.
2. Get as close as possible to your subject – the camera's red-eye reduction works more effectively at close range.
3. With zoom compacts, use the lens at wide-angle rather than telephoto distance, because the lens aperture is faster and you will be nearer to the subject.
4. Switch the lights on when shooting indoors. This reduces the size of the subject's pupils prior to taking the shot.
5. Use a fast film; ISO 400 is recommended. Faster film speeds require less flash.
6. Ask the subject to look at a bright light source just before taking the picture as this will contract the pupils.

C This portrait of a young girl, taken with flash at a night-time celebration, was highly likely to display some red eye. Selecting the camera's red-eye reduction mode for the second picture has eliminated the problem.

The advanced photo system

Although this format has been around for only a few years, it has had a dramatic effect on the compact camera market. Here we examine the features of this system and how they can help you to overcome some of the common pitfalls associated with standard 35mm compacts.

The Advanced Photo System (APS) was launched in 1996 by a consortium of five companies (Canon, Fuji, Kodak, Minolta and Nikon). Research by this group of five, known as the System Developing Companies (SDC), had found that thousands of 35mm films were spoilt each year due to simple mistakes, such as loading the film incorrectly.

It was decided that it was not feasible to adapt 35mm films to overcome this problem. Instead, a new film format was

developed that avoided the shortfalls of 35mm and also took on board the latest advances in technology. APS is steadily increasing its share of the compact camera market and there's no doubt that this new format is here to stay. In fact, it's quite likely that in a few years time APS will be the dominant compact camera film format. Some manufacturers have even gone as far as to say that they will cease producing 35mm compacts completely, in favour of APS models.

↻ Loading a film into an APS compact is very easy. Open the film compartment door, drop the film cassette in, close the door and you're ready to start taking pictures.

THE ADVANTAGES OF APS
Drop-in loading
This has helped to solve one of the most common problems associated with 35mm cameras – difficulty in loading film. Because there is no film leader, loading an APS film simply involves dropping the film cassette into the film compartment and closing the cover. There is only one way to insert the film cassette into the camera, making film loading easy.

Information Exchange (IX)
A magnetic strip on the film records exposure data from the camera and passes this on to the processing equipment to improve print quality.

Smaller film cassettes
Because APS film is smaller than 35mm, the cameras can be made smaller and lighter than 35mm models.

Status indicator
The top of the APS film cassette has the following visual indicators to show at a glance whether the film has been used, thus preventing you from using the same film more than once.
● The film is unused
◗ The film is partly used
✖ The film has been used but not processed
■ The film has been processed

Mid-roll Change (MRC)
Many compact cameras offer this facility, which allows you to rewind and remove a partly used film. The really clever part with APS comes when you reload the film

Index Print
Photos are returned with an Index Print, a sheet with numbered thumbnail prints of all the photos on the film. Each thumbnail has a frame number which relates to the number on the APS negative, making ordering reprints of pictures easy. An ID number on the index print matches a number on the film so there's no reason to send the wrong film off.

at a later date, because it is automatically advanced to the next unexposed frame.

Storage of negatives within cassette

The film always stays within the cassette (except when loaded in the camera or during processing). This ensures that the negatives do not get damaged or scratched. When you require reprints, you need only to look at the Index Print, note the number of the picture to be reprinted, and hand this over with the cassette to the processing lab.

Three print formats

APS cameras offer the choice of three different print formats, selected by moving a switch on the camera: Classic, 6x4in (152x100mm); HDTV, 7x4in (178x100mm); and Panoramic, 10x4in (254x100mm).

APS FILM

APS film is 40 per cent smaller than standard 35mm film, with an image size measuring 30x17mm compared to 36x24mm. In theory, this should mean that image quality from APS film is inferior to that from 35mm, with prints exhibiting larger grain and less sharpness. However, the APS film companies have developed a new emulsion to counter these problems. The base of APS film is made of a chemical known as Annealed-Polyethylens Naphthalate (A-PEN) which is stronger than its 35mm equivalent yet 30 per cent thinner. The film grain has also been improved by making it smaller, and improving sharpness.

As a result of these developments it is now difficult to spot the difference

Top tip
- You can change the status indicator, if, for instance, you have rewound a partly used film by mistake. This involves squeezing the inner spool at each end of the cassette and turning it until the indicator has moved from the number three (used but not processed) position back to the number one (unused) position.

⋒ HDTV
⋐ Panoramic
↻ Classic

These three pictures show the different sizes of the APS print formats.

The **Classic format (C)** matches the dimensions of a standard 35mm print and is useful for tight composition, as in this shot of a person framed by a hole in an old wall.

The **HDTV format (H)** is useful when photographing large objects or groups. The extra width of this format made it the perfect choice for capturing this herd of elephants.

The **Panoramic format (P)** is ideal for landscapes or for making the most of long, narrow subjects such as this theme park ride.

between a pair of similarly sized prints, one shot on 35mm film and the other on APS.

Information exchange (IX)

As has already been mentioned, APS film uses a magnetic strip to record information which is then read by the processing equipment. As well as mid-roll change and print format selection, other features of information exchange are:

DATE AND TIME IMPRINTING This prints the date and time on your photos. Some cameras allow you to print this

Focal-length comparison

The smaller image area of APS means that compared to the 35mm format, APS lenses need a shorter focal length to achieve the same magnification.

To calculate the 35mm equivalent, multiply the APS focal length by x1.25. For instance, a 24mm lens on an APS camera has the same angle of view as a 30mm lens on a 35mm film camera.

Focal lengths - APS v 35mm

This comparison table shows the most common focal lengths.

APS format	35mm format
24mm	30mm
30mm	38mm
50mm	62mm
75mm	94mm
90mm	112mm
100mm	125mm
120mm	150mm

information on either the front or back of your prints.

PRINT QUALITY IMPROVEMENT (PQI) Cameras with this feature record exposure information, such as flash use, magnetically on the film. The idea is that the processing machines at the developers can use this information to produce better quality results.

PRINT QUANTITY (PQ) This feature lets you decide how many copies of a print you would like before you take the picture. So, if you're taking a photo at a birthday party and you know five relatives would like reprints, you set the PQ number to six, and when the pictures are returned, you already have an extra five reprints ready for everyone else. The camera will automatically switch off the facility after one shot. Some compacts even allow you to change the print quantity after you have taken the picture.

TITLING Cameras with this feature store a number of messages, such as 'Happy Birthday', which can be printed on the photograph in a number of languages.

Print formats

Having three different print formats makes picture-taking easier and more versatile because you are able to vary the choice of format to suit the subject.

You will find that some subjects benefit from a particular print format. For instance, the Panoramic size suits sweeping landscapes, whereas group shots benefit from the extra width offered by the HDTV format.

If you have your pictures returned and wish you'd taken them in a different format, there's no need to worry. All you need to do is have the photo reprinted and indicate which format you require. This is because every photograph is always recorded full frame but IX notes which format was selected and informs the processor to print that particular size.

APS ON TV

Some manufacturers have developed Photo players which allow you to view APS pictures on your TV. All you have to do is pop your processed APS cassette into the player and you're then able to present your own picture show. The Photo players also allow you to add titles and music, as well as zoom in to highlight particular parts of the frame. ■

↻ The Pentax efina has a 24–48mm zoom and features a large mode dial which makes it particularly easy to use.

Q&A: APS

Does the smaller film size of APS compared to 35mm mean that prints from APS film aren't as good as those from 35mm?
The APS film emulsion has been developed so that it offers better quality than 35mm. When you enlarge the negative to produce a print, you will find that there is no noticeable difference in quality between 35mm and APS films.

How many exposures are there on an APS film?
APS cassettes are available with 15, 25 or 40 exposures.

Is it possible to use APS film in a 35mm camera?
No. The two film formats are not compatible.

What types of film are available for APS?
Initially, only colour print film was available in APS. However, it is now possible to buy black-and-white print film and colour slide film in the APS format.

Where do I get APS film processed?
Most high-street photo labs, and some mail-order companies, offer an APS processing service. Film and processing tends to be slightly more expensive than for 35mm.

The digital camera

Rather than using film, digital cameras store images electronically. This has the advantage of allowing instant access to pictures, as well as saving on the cost of buying and processing film. The new 'megapixel' digital cameras are now capable of producing high-resolution images.

Digital cameras are as easy to use as compact cameras – all you need to do is switch them on, point and shoot. Then the pictures can be transferred from the camera to a computer via the appropriate cable. Some cameras allow pictures to be transferred directly to a printer.

Although at first glance most digital cameras look similar to 35mm or APS cameras, they have some of the following unique features.

THE MAIN FEATURES
Lens

The lens of a digital camera is similar to that found on a 35mm or APS camera, except that the focal length is much shorter. In most cases, multiplying the focal length of a digital camera by seven gives an equivalent value to 35mm cameras. For example, 6mm on a digital camera is roughly the same as 42mm on a 35mm camera.

FRONT VIEW

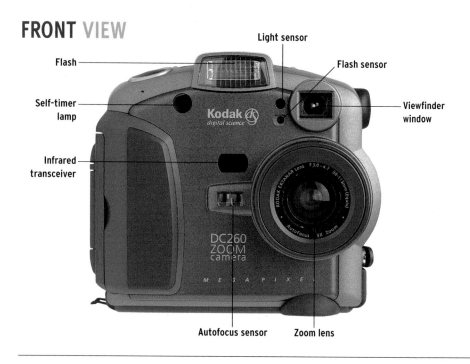

Light sensor

Flash

Flash sensor

Self-timer lamp

Viewfinder window

Infrared transceiver

DC260 ZOOM camera

M E G A P I X E L

Autofocus sensor

Zoom lens

TOP VIEW

Zoom lens

Flash

LCD panel

Shutter-release button

Menu buttons

Self timer

On/off switch

REAR VIEW

Viewfinder

LED indicator

Zoom control

LCD screen

Menu buttons

Microphone

Audio record button

Menu buttons

Multi-function button

Built-in flash

The low power of the built-in flash means that it is suitable only for subjects within a few metres of the camera. Most cameras feature autoflash in low light or backlit conditions. Many cameras feature a red-eye reduction facility, although this isn't strictly necessary, as any red eye can easily be removed during image editing on the computer (see page 202).

Metering and focusing sensors

Sensors help produce sharp and well-exposed pictures. Some cameras offer a TTL (Through The Lens) system to work out the exposure and focus.

Self-timer lamp

This lights up when the self-timer is engaged, and flashes just before the picture is taken.

LCD monitor

This provides a 'live' image – similar to a small TV screen – so you can see how it looks before you shoot. You can also use the monitor to review pictures you have already taken, so you can free up memory space by deleting unwanted shots. Some cameras, such as the Kodak DC260, have an on-screen menu for easy operation.

Optical viewfinder

The viewfinder is almost identical to the type found on compact cameras. It has an advantage over the LCD monitor in that it doesn't drain any battery power. Most optical viewfinders have one or two lamps beside them to show that the flash is fully recharged and/or the autofocus is locked onto the subject.

Mode dial

This lets you switch the camera from taking pictures (often called 'record' mode) to reviewing images in the camera's memory ('play' mode).

Zoom control

This allows you to change the focal length of the zoom lens from wide-angle (W) to telephoto (T).

Connection socket

This is where the cable that transfers the pictures from the camera to the computer is connected.

Mains socket

Digital cameras, especially those with LCD monitors, consume battery power quickly, so many feature a socket to allow the connection of a mains adaptor when used indoors.

IMAGE CAPTURE
The CCD

A digital camera doesn't use film. Instead, the image is captured on a charge-coupled device (CCD), a light-sensitive chip that converts light into an electrical signal. The CCD is made up of thousands of individual sensors, sensitive to either green, blue or red light. Because the human eye is more sensitive to green than any other colour, there are more green-sensitive sensors than red or blue. These sensors are also commonly known as picture elements, or pixels. Various types of CCD are available, including some that use red, green and blue filters to obtain colour information, but each conforms to this basic principle of image capture.

Image storage

Because digital cameras do not use film, they store the images internally on one of the following types of memory:

Internal memory

Images are stored on the camera's internal memory. When it is full, additional storage space becomes available only when unwanted images are erased. Cameras storing photos on internal memory are comparatively cheap compared to those using memory cards (see below). However, they are restricted by the limited number of images that can be stored.

Removable memory cards

Memory cards (also called storage cards) have the advantage that when one becomes full, you can remove it and replace it with an empty one. As long as you keep one or two spare cards, you will always have some memory free for extra photos. There are several different formats of card, each with a range of memory sizes.

SmartMedia cards are very slim and relatively cheap but the maximum storage is less than with other formats. Cards of at least 32Mb will soon become available but may not be compatible with existing cameras using SmartMedia cards. SmartMedia was developed by Toshiba and is used by Agfa, Fuji, Olympus and Minolta.

CompactFlash cards are more expensive than SmartMedia but are thicker, more robust and offer a higher maximum capacity (currently 96Mb), with higher capacities to follow. CompactFlash is supported by Canon, Casio, Kodak and Hewlett-Packard. **PCMCIA cards** are used by some high-end cameras and come in three versions. Types I and II are known as flash memory cards and go up to a capacity of 175Mb. The type III hard disk card currently has a capacity of 1040Mb.

Floppy disks

Currently used only by the Sony Mavica range of cameras, these do away with the need to download the images from camera to computer. They are extremely convenient but the floppy disk format limits how many pictures can be saved on a disk.

꙳ Removable memory cards: CompactFlash (left); PCMCIA (centre); and SmartMedia (right)

CCD sensitivity

This is usually specified in the same way as with film, by being given an equivalent ISO rating. During an exposure, the CCD develops a charge, and the greater the exposure, the higher the charge. If a CCD element receives too much exposure, the highlights will bleach and spread the charge to adjacent elements, resulting in 'blooming'. If CCD elements do not receive light, there is a small build up of background charge known as 'noise', which may result in incorrectly coloured pixels in the shadows.

Image resolution

The resolution of digital cameras is usually quoted as the number of horizontal pixels multiplied by the number of vertical pixels. For instance, a resolution of 1024x768 pixels means a total of over 786,000 pixels. The more pixels there are, the higher the resolution. Most cameras can capture the image in different resolutions, usually shown as high, normal or low. This is usually achieved by using image compression (see opposite).

Interpolation

This method increases the apparent resolution by using software to create extra pixels and assigning colours and densities to them. This works well but excessive use results in blurred edges and an overall loss of sharpness.

Resolution comparison

These three images were taken at various resolutions to show the difference in quality.

1536 x 1024
A very high resolution records an excellent amount of detail and produces very accurate colours and a wide range of tones.

1152 x 768
Although this resolution is relatively high, there is a drop in sharpness and less detail, which becomes more obvious upon magnification.

768 x 512
A lower resolution results in the image appearing less sharp with a noticeable loss of detail and less accurate colour reproduction.

Image compression

Storing digital pictures takes up memory and the higher the resolution of the image, the more memory is required. A picture made up of 1024x768 pixels, for example, requires just over two megabytes of memory. To allow more pictures to be saved the images are compressed by reducing their file size.

There are two main types of compression – 'lossless' and 'lossy'. Lossless compression organizes the way a picture is stored in a more efficient way, so the image takes up less storage space without any loss in quality. One of the most common types of lossless compression is called LZW compression.

Lossy compression is not quite as refined, and works on the principle that the human eye cannot perceive all the colours in a picture. Lossy compression frees up memory by searching a picture and erasing any unnecessary colours. It is possible to specify how much lossy compression should occur; small levels may not affect image quality, but higher levels will result in a drop in quality.

Image formats

The digital picture can be stored in a number of image formats, with the two most popular being TIFF (Tagged Image File Format), which is widely used in desktop publishing, and JPEG (Joint Photographic Experts Group), which takes up very little storage space and uses a lossy compression technique with the amount of compression being set by the user. JPEG is also the standard image format if you want to put pictures onto the Internet.

Q&A: Digital cameras

Why is there a delay between the picture being taken and the camera storing it in its memory?

When the shutter release is pressed, the CCD converts the light into an electrical pulse which is converted in the camera into a digital signal. But this information can't be recorded all at once, so a software program holds and transfers the data to the camera's memory in stages.

What's the point of using a low-resolution camera or using a lossy compression system?

The resolution is good enough to view on computer screens and so is suitable for viewing on the Internet or for sending pictures by e-mail. The pictures also have enough detail for use at a small size, making them ideal for commercial uses such as ID cards, catalogues, computer databases, or for small photos in classified advertisements.

Is it possible to get decent quality prints from a digital camera?

Yes. There are a growing number of inkjet printers designed for use with home computers that are capable of producing photo-realistic prints. The resolution of the camera must be as high as possible, however, especially if you want to produce a large print.

THE MAIN TYPES OF DIGITAL CAMERA

Digital cameras are manufactured in many shapes and sizes. They can be divided into groups, according to the resolution at which the camera captures the image.

Low-resolution cameras

These cameras offer a low resolution of 320x240 pixels, making them unsuitable for serious photographic applications. However, the resolution is acceptable for producing pictures to be used on the Internet. So as long as you don't expect photographic-quality results, these low-cost cameras can be a good way to try out digital photography.

Medium-resolution cameras

The majority of consumer digital cameras come in this section of the market. This group is made up of cameras with resolutions ranging from 640x480 pixels (known as VGA – Video Graphics Array cameras) to 800x600 pixels (SVGA – Super VGA cameras), and 1024x768 pixels (XGA – Extended GA cameras). These types of cameras are capable of producing postcard-sized prints of acceptable quality.

High-resolution cameras

Cameras in this category are often given the tag 'megapixel', and are becoming increasingly popular. This means that the camera boasts a resolution of at least one million pixels. The photos produced from this class of camera are suitable for

1: Medium-resolution digital camera
2-4: High-resolution digital cameras
5: High-resolution single-lens reflex digital camera

printing up to A4 in size, and show excellent definition and colour reproduction. Despite their high performance, megapixel cameras are becoming much more affordable, making them excellent value for money.

High-resolution single-lens reflex cameras

A single-lens reflex (SLR) is a type of camera that uses an advanced optical system to show the exact image that the lens is viewing through the viewfinder. This allows for more precise framing of the subject. Currently, there are few digital SLRs on the market, but those that are available boast zoom lenses and very high resolutions. ■

Professional high-resolution single-lens reflex cameras

These are 35mm or APS single-lens reflex cameras with interchangeable lenses that have been adapted for digital use and are therefore very expensive. Designed for professional applications, these offer an extremely high resolution, ranging on average from two to six million pixels, good enough images for publication in newspapers and magazines. These cameras require powerful computers to handle the large file sizes of the photographs and are mainly used by press photographers covering news stories or sporting events. Pictures are usually transmitted via a mobile phone and laptop computer so that the pictures can be received within minutes of being taken.

④

⑤

Lenses

The lens is the 'eye' of the camera and is the single most important feature in determining the quality of the picture. There is a lens to suit every conceivable situation, and understanding how different lenses will affect the image is a key part of successful photography.

Light must pass through the lens to form an image, so the better the lens, the higher the resolution of the image. In the past, plastic lenses were inferior to glass and were usually found only in budget cameras, but improvements in the manufacture of plastic have led to their widespread use, although glass is still used for the highest optical quality. The quality of the lenses in some compact cameras is so high that the results compare to those of professional cameras.

FOCAL LENGTH AND ANGLE OF VIEW

The focal length of a lens is measured in millimetres and determines how much of the subject is included in the frame. The wider the focal length, the wider the angle of view and the more of the scene included in the frame.

The angle of view of the human eye is 46 degrees and equates to a 50mm lens. A lens that has a wider angle of view than the human eye (and therefore includes more of the scene in the frame) is known as a wide-angle lens. A lens that has a narrower angle of view than the human eye (including less of the scene, but magnifying detail) is called a telephoto lens.

Some focal lengths are more suitable for particular subjects, and knowing which type of lens is most appropriate for a specific shot will significantly improve your photography.

WIDE-ANGLE LENSES are the perfect choice for including a large area of a scene in the frame. This makes them suitable for subjects such as landscapes, architecture and group shots. The

↻ Ultra wide-angle lenses such as a 16mm not only feature an extremely wide angle of view but also lead to an effect known as distortion. This causes straight lines to appear as curves on the photograph and can result in some unusual results, as seen in this shot of a Ferrari monument displaying severe bending at its base.

majority of compacts with wide-angle lenses feature a 28mm or 35mm focal length. Ultra wide-angle lenses with a focal length of 16mm or 21mm are available for a select number of expensive compacts, such as the Contax G2. **TELEPHOTO LENSES** concentrate on a smaller part of the scene, making things

look closer than they really are. These are ideal if you can't get close to the subject but want it to appear large in the frame. Short telephoto lenses (up to 105mm) are perfect for portraits as they produce a very flattering result. Longer focal lengths are available for magnifying distant subjects, such as wildlife.

➲ The Pentax Espio 200 offers the most powerful telephoto zoom currently found on a compact camera – an impressive 48–200mm.

Angle of view

This diagram shows the angle of view of lenses with focal lengths from 16mm to 400mm.

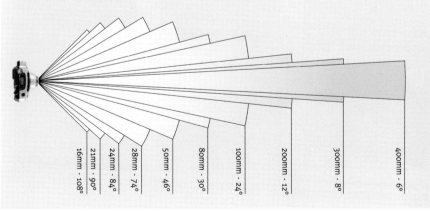

16mm - 108°
21mm - 90°
24mm - 84°
28mm - 74°
50mm - 46°
80mm - 30°
100mm - 24°
200mm - 12°
300mm - 8°
400mm - 6°

Focal length comparison

The pictures in this series were all taken from the same spot and show the angle of view of different focal lengths. Remember, 50mm offers an angle of view similar to that of the human eye. A focal length offering a wider angle of view than 50mm is known as wide-angle, anything with a narrower angle of view is referred to as telephoto. The wider the angle of view, the smaller subjects appear in the frame; while an increase in focal length results in a smaller part of the frame being magnified to a greater extent.

16mm – 108 degrees This ultra wide-angle lens has captured the widest area of the scene but this focal length is available on only a few top-quality rangefinder cameras.

21mm – 90 degrees

24mm – 84 degrees

28mm – 74 degrees

50mm – 46 degrees

80mm – 30 degrees

100mm – 24 degrees

200mm – 12 degrees

300mm – 8 degrees

400mm – 6 degrees

TYPES OF LENS

Lenses can be divided into two main types – fixed and zoom. Each has its own advantages and disadvantages which are discussed below.

Fixed lens

A fixed lens has only one focal length, usually a wide-angle, such as 28mm or 35mm.

Its main advantages are:

1. Cameras are usually smaller, lighter and cheaper than models with zooms.

2. The optical quality of the lens is usually better than with a similarly priced camera with a zoom.

3. The maximum aperture of a fixed lens is wider than on a zoom, thus reducing the risk of camera shake and making the lens more suitable for low-light photography.

The main disadvantage of a fixed lens is that framing the subject requires the photographer to physically move towards or away from it.

Zoom lens

The focal length of a zoom lens can usually be adjusted from a wide-angle to a short telephoto setting. Most zoom compact cameras offer a range of around 38–80mm, although models with 38–115mm zooms are not uncommon. Improvements in lens design and manufacture in recent years mean that the optical quality is now virtually indistinguishable from that of a fixed lens.

The main advantages are:

1. A zooms lens is more suitable for distant subjects, because the telephoto setting magnifies the subject.

2. There is greater versatility for framing the subject. Rather than physically moving, you can simply zoom the lens to frame the subject.

The main disadvantages are:

1. Most zoom compacts are bulkier, heavier and more expensive than fixed-lens models.

2. The smaller maximum aperture of a zoom lens means that a faster film is required to avoid camera shake, especially in low-light conditions. ■

⌁ Although very close to the horse, the wide angle of view of a 21mm wide-angle lens allowed the entire subject to fit into the frame. It's a useful focal length to have if you want to take pictures in a confined space such as a small room.

⌒ A 50mm lens has an angle of view similar to that of the human eye and can be used for various applications, ranging from portraits to general scenes such as this shot of a moored fishing boat.

⟳ Telephoto lenses with focal lengths of over 100mm are great for filling the frame with distant subjects. This tennis umpire was photographed at 200mm, and although a fair distance from the camera, he fills the frame because of the powerful magnification of the lens.

Top tips

- If you're using a zoom compact, it's worth zooming through the entire focal length before taking a picture.

- Always keep the lens cap on when the camera is not in use.

↷ Lenses with a focal length between 50mm and 100mm are often referred to as short telephotos. They are an excellent choice for portraits or for isolating details in architecture.

↻ This shot of the Explorer Space Shuttle was taken with a wide-angle focal length of 28mm. It's a fairly common focal length on compact cameras and a good choice if you enjoy photographing landscapes.

Q&A: Lenses

What is the most powerful zoom lens on a compact or digital camera?

At the time of writing, the most powerful zoom on a 35mm compact is the 48-200mm zoom on the Pentax Espio 200. The Minolta Vectis 40 boasts a 30-120mm zoom (equivalent to 38-150mm in the 35mm format). The Sony Mavica MVD-FD91 digital camera takes the honours with a zoom equivalent to 37-518mm in the 35mm format.

Is a lens made up of one single piece of glass or plastic?

No. Lenses are far more complex than that. A lens is made up of several 'elements', which are arranged in 'groups'. Many lenses include glass and plastic elements in their construction.

How should I clean the lens?

To prevent scratching the surface of the lens, use a microfibre cloth to wipe dirt and smears from the surface. These are available from most opticians.

My camera features a screw thread around the lens. What is this for?

Some compacts allow screw-on filters to be attached in front of the lens. This facility opens up a number of creative possibilities such as using infrared film (which requires a filter). For more information on filters see pages 74-75.

Focusing systems

The camera's focusing system is crucial to the sharpness of the photograph. Most modern cameras feature sophisticated autofocusing that detects how far away the subject is and adjusts the lens automatically, giving you more time to respond to photo opportunities.

This section looks at the three main types of focusing systems: fixed focus, autofocus and manual focus.

FIXED FOCUS

This is the simplest method, as the lens does not adjust the focus, regardless of how far the subject is from the camera. Instead, the lens relies on depth-of-field to produce pictures that display reasonable sharpness.

Fixed-focus lenses are found on most compact cameras at the budget end of the price range, such as single-use cameras.

AUTOFOCUS (AF)

For good quality pictures, you should consider an autofocus compact camera. Because the lens adjusts its focus according to the subject distance, photographs are much sharper than those taken with a fixed-focus lens. And the great advantage of having the camera take care of the focusing is that it gives you one thing less to think about, allowing you to react quickly when a good photo opportunity presents itself. You can then concentrate on the composition of the picture and making sure your subject is suitably posed.

There are two main methods of autofocusing in compact cameras – active and passive. With the active system, the camera emits an infrared beam which bounces off the subject. Sensors on the front of the camera detect the reflected beam and determine how far away the subject is.

With the passive system, the focusing works by detecting differences in the subject's contrast to calculate the focusing distance. In other words, the camera looks for changes in the tone, colour or texture of the subject in order to determine the subject's distance. For instance, imagine you have two identical cameras, one pointing at a plain wall, the other at a wall covered in striped wallpaper. The camera aimed at the plain wall will have difficulty calculating the focusing distance because it is unable to detect any changes on the wall's surface. The camera pointing to the striped wall will not encounter the same difficulties, however, as it can detect changes in the contrast of the stripes to work out the focusing distance.

The accuracy of the AF system is determined by the number of focusing steps it uses. When the camera detects the subject, it sets the lens to the closest focusing step. Therefore the more focusing steps the system uses, the more accurate the AF.

Say you are photographing a subject that is two and a half metres away from you, for example. Camera A has focusing steps at one metre, five metres and ten metres; camera B has focusing steps at one metre, two metres, five metres and ten metres. While camera A will set the lens to one metre, camera B will be able to set the lens to two metres, resulting in a much sharper picture because the lens can focus closer to the subject.

Some compacts feature several hundred focusing steps, with most of the steps found at very close distances where accuracy is most important.

Focusing points

Up until the last few years, all AF compacts had one focusing point at the centre of the frame. As long as the subject was in the centre, it would be focused correctly. However, if the picture was composed with the main subject to one side of the frame, the background would come out sharp while the subject would be out of focus.

One solution to this problem is the focus-lock facility. Positioning the subject in the centre of the frame and pressing the shutter button halfway 'locks' the focus. With the button kept at this position, you can recompose the scene with the main subject to the side. In

↻ The only way the photographer could get a picture of this street entertainer was to take it through the crowd. In this situation, the multi-point focus would have locked onto the backs of the heads of the people in front, and the entertainer would have been out of focus. However, using the spot AF facility (see page 45) has meant that the main subject is sharp while the crowd is out of focus.

Differential focus

This technique involves focusing on a part of the scene to pay it particular attention. Usually this is to make a subject in the foreground stand out from the background or vice versa.

These two images were both taken from exactly the same position, but by focusing on different points, the photographer has been able to draw attention to particular parts of the scene.

➲ For the first shot, the focus was locked on the fin at the front of the car and has thrown the background completely out of focus.

↻ For the second picture, focus was on the front end of the car at the top of the frame. This has brought the background into focus and thrown the car in the foreground out of focus.

theory this system works perfectly, but in practice it is difficult to keep the button held in this position. The photographer may release the button accidentally or depress it fully. To overcome this problem, most manufacturers now produce compacts boasting multiple focusing points. The most common number of focusing points is three, but some compacts boast up to seven. This increases the success rate of taking properly focused pictures of off-centre subjects by having focusing points positioned across the frame. When the shutter button is depressed, the camera checks all the focusing points and is able to detect where the subject is.

↻ The servo AF facility of most compacts can handle slow-moving subjects but anything faster can present problems. This cyclist was moving at a constant speed towards the photographer.

Spot AF

Many cameras with multi-point focusing offer a feature known as spot AF. Using this facility switches the camera's autofocus system to the central focusing point only. This feature is useful in situations where you want the camera to focus on the subject at the centre of the frame but there are off-centre objects closer to the camera that the AF system may focus on.

This system is especially useful if you are trying to take pictures through a crowd, or your subject is partially obscured by other objects. Spot AF is ideal if you are trying to photograph someone standing in between but just slightly behind a pair of pillars.

The spot AF facility is also very effective when shooting close-ups because it allows you to isolate a particular subject. If you are photographing a bunch of flowers, for instance, using spot AF will enable you to isolate one flower or even a small section of an individual flower.

Servo AF

More advanced cameras offer a feature known as servo AF. This allows the autofocus system to keep track of a moving subject and keep it in focus. It's a system that works well for slow-moving subjects, but shouldn't be expected to cope with anything moving at speed.

Servo AF works best with subjects that are moving at a constant speed and in the same direction. So if you are trying to take a photograph of a child riding a bicycle, for instance, it is best to wait until they're moving at a fairly regular speed, either towards you or across the frame. Where servo systems do encounter difficulties is when the speed of the subject is erratic or the subject keeps changing direction.

MANUAL FOCUS

This is a secondary option, found only on a handful of autofocus compacts, which allows you to set the focusing distance manually if the camera's autofocus system is having difficulties.

You don't actually turn the lens physically to adjust focus. It's all done using electronics. The LCD on the camera displays a distance range and you adjust the focus setting using a button or dial until the preferred distance is selected. The camera sets the focus when you press the shutter button. Cameras offering this feature tend to be luxury models such as the Contax G2. ■

↻ Snow can present problems for a camera's focusing system because it lacks contrast. However, you can overcome this problem by looking for variations in the tone or texture of the snow, or focusing on any rocky outcrops or trees in the scene.

Autofocus systems

Autofocus systems aren't perfect and can be fooled in particular shooting conditions. The following situations may cause problems for your camera's AF, resulting in a blurred picture unless the appropriate solution is taken:

1. Low-contrast subjects

Point the camera at a very plain subject, such as a white wall, and it will not be able to detect it.

2. Fast-moving subjects

By the time the camera's autofocus has managed to lock onto the subject and the shutter has fired, the subject will have moved position.

3. Subjects partly hidden behind another object

Some subjects, such as a zoo animal in a cage, are difficult to shoot because other things – in this instance, the cage bars – interfere with focusing.

4. Reflective surfaces

The autofocus system is unable to lock onto highly reflective subjects such as snow or shiny metal.

5. Low-light situations

Autofocus systems need light to help them lock onto the subject. They are sometimes unable to work properly at night, or in a dark room.

6. Shooting through glass

Active AF systems have major problems shooting through glass, as the infrared beams reflect back off the surface.

The solutions:

1, 3 and 4. Focus-lock on a subject a similar distance away, then recompose and shoot.
2. Focus-lock on the ground at a particular spot and fully depress the shutter button when the subject is just about to reach that point.
5. Turn the room light on if you are shooting indoors. For outdoor shots, try to position your subject in an area where there is better light, or focus on a well-lit object a similar distance away.
6. Point the camera at an angle to the glass or use the camera's infinity lock function, if it has one.

ↄ Zoo enclosures are often surrounded by glass, making it difficult to get a good shot of the animal. Pointing the camera at an angle to the glass, in this case downwards, helped the autofocus system lock onto the head of the polar bear.

Exposure

In simple terms, a photograph is the result of exposing light-sensitive material (film in a 35mm or APS compact, or the CCD in a digital camera) to light. The amount of light reaching the film – the exposure – has to be correct, otherwise the image will be incorrectly exposed.

METERING SYSTEMS

A correct exposure results in a photograph having the same range and intensity of tone as the scene being photographed.

In compact cameras using film, too much light results in too many silver grains being exposed, a term known as overexposure. Too little light, and not enough silver atoms are exposed, resulting in underexposure. In digital cameras, underexposure occurs when the pixels do not receive enough light and overexposure occurs when the pixels receive too much light.

Autoexposure cameras have made setting the correct exposure much easier. Sensors on the camera measure the amount of light reflecting back off the subject, and the camera uses this information to calculate the exposure – a process known as metering. The sensors that measure the light level are found at the front of most cameras, although some cameras measure the light through the lens, a system known as TTL metering.

Calculating exposure

So how does a camera work out the exposure? All metering systems are calibrated to expose a scene correctly with an average reflectance of 18 per cent grey. This means that the metering system measures the scene and attempts to set an exposure that will result in the subject appearing 18 per cent grey. It has been calculated that averaging out all the tones in a typical scene results in this value, so calibrating the metering system to a value of 18 per cent grey will therefore produce a high rate of good quality images. Colours similar in density to 18 per cent

C Although the head of this dog is mostly black, including the white fur of its neck in the frame has averaged out the tones and resulted in the camera's meter producing a perfect exposure.

grey are often referred to as mid-tones, and include green foliage, brown brickwork or grey concrete.

Unfortunately, not every scene averages out to this figure. A white wall, for example, will reflect almost all the light falling on it, while a jet-black subject will reflect little light. This means that perfect exposures cannot be guaranteed every time. Nonetheless, the accuracy of current metering systems should not be underestimated.

The two main types of metering systems used in compact and digital cameras are 'centre-weighted average metering' and 'multi-zone metering'. Many cameras also feature an extra option called 'spot metering'. Each metering system calculates exposure differently, and has its own advantages and disadvantages.

Centre-weighted average metering

This type of metering system has been in use on all types of cameras for several decades. The meter takes an average of the entire frame but gives most emphasis to the central area of the frame. The system works well in most situations, but has problems with very bright and dark scenes, and also with backlit subjects. Another failing of this system is that it tends to underexpose the frame if a large area of sky is included in the shot.

Multi-zone metering

Multi-zone metering is a sophisticated system that is becoming increasingly common in cameras. The frame is divided into a number of zones and an exposure reading is taken for each zone. The

⌒ For normal shooting conditions, in full sunlight, centre-weighted average metering can be relied upon to produce the correct exposure.

camera uses these individual readings to calculate the overall exposure. Multi-zone metering has a high success rate because the camera is able to analyse its readings using data stored in its memory and set the exposure accordingly. Multi-zone metering can cope with many more situations than centre-weighted average metering, although it, too, can encounter problems with backlit subjects.

Spot metering

Spot metering is a secondary option on many of the more expensive models. This system tests a very small part of the area in the centre of the frame, producing

SPOT METERING

Top: Taking a reading from the black subject has led to severe overexposure, as the meter has attempted to record it as 18 per cent grey.
Centre: Metering from the white subject has had the opposite effect, and has led to underexposure.
Bottom: Taking a reading from the mid-toned background has produced the correct result, with both the black and white chesspieces correctly exposed.

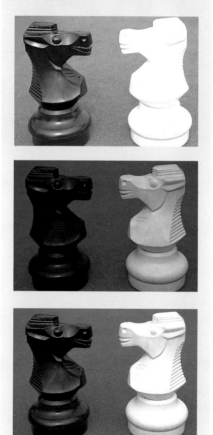

precise readings. Spot metering is best used in very tricky lighting situations, such as backlighting. You need to use the system with care, however. Take a reading from a light or dark subject and the exposure will be incorrect. Instead, meter off a mid-tone, such as concrete or a grey road surface. If you're in a rural area, take a spot meter off the grass.

The correct exposure

We've looked at how the meter calculates the exposure, but how does the camera physically interpret this information?

For light to reach the film (or CCD in a digital camera), it must first pass through the lens. In the lens is an iris, similar to the one in a human eye, that controls

☊ Strongly backlit subjects present problems for a camera's exposure system. Taking a spot reading from a mid-tone, in this case the face of the horse trainer, has produced an accurate exposure.

↻ Bright blue sky in the background usually causes a centre-weighted metering system to underexpose the picture. However, the more sophisticated multi-zone system is able to handle most difficult lighting conditions and produces a very high rate of correctly exposed pictures.

Top tip

■ On cameras with multi-point focusing, the spot-metering facility also switches the autofocus system to the central area of the frame, because the camera assumes you are taking a spot-meter reading from the main subject.

Q&A: Metering

How do I avoid the problems of over- or underexposure?

Use the spot meter facility (if available) and take a reading off a mid-tone. If your camera has exposure compensation add exposure for light and reflective subjects, and reduce exposure for dark subjects. If your camera doesn't have any form of exposure override, you should take a reading from a mid-toned subject.

How many metering segments are there in a multi-zone pattern?

This varies, but there are usually three to five zones. The general rule is that the more zones the pattern has, the more accurate the system.

the amount of light passing through. The length of time the light has to pass through this aperture is determined by the shutter speed. The longer the shutter stays open, the more light is able to pass through.

The widest aperture setting of the lens iris is referred to as the maximum aperture, the smallest setting is known as the minimum aperture. By controlling the size of the aperture (using the aperture setting) and the amount of time the shutter stays open (the shutter speed), the camera is able to control the exposure. The correct exposure is achieved by getting the right relationship between the aperture and shutter speed.

APERTURE SETTINGS AND SHUTTER SPEEDS

Apertures

The size of the aperture is shown as an f/number. The larger the aperture, the lower the f/number. A standard sequence of aperture values is as follows: f/1, f/1.4, f/2, f/2.8, f/4, f/5.6, f/8, f/11, f/16, f/22, f/32. Each stage of this sequence represents a halving of the amount of light passing through the aperture. For instance, f/4 allows twice as much light through as f/5.6, but only half the light of f/2.8. Each stage of the sequence (each halving or doubling of the exposure) is known as a 'stop'.

Shutter speeds

These are measured in seconds, or more accurately, fractions of a second. A standard sequence of shutter speeds is as follows: 1sec, ½sec, ¼sec, ⅛sec, $\frac{1}{15}$sec, $\frac{1}{30}$sec, $\frac{1}{60}$sec, $\frac{1}{125}$sec, $\frac{1}{250}$sec, $\frac{1}{500}$sec, $\frac{1}{1000}$sec and

so on. As with apertures, each stage is called a 'stop', and represents a halving or doubling of the amount of light passing through.

The right combination

By obtaining the right combination of aperture setting and shutter speed, the camera is able to produce the correct exposure. There is more than one aperture/shutter speed combination available for producing a correct exposure. Imagine, for example, that $\frac{1}{250}$sec at f/8 produces the correct exposure. A combination of $\frac{1}{125}$sec at f/11, or $\frac{1}{500}$sec at f/5.6 will produce exactly the same exposure, as each change in the aperture has been counteracted by a change in the shutter speed.

Film-speed rating

Another factor in determining the choice of shutter speed/aperture combination is the ISO rating (speed) of the film inside the camera. With compacts, the general rule is the faster the film speed (with a higher ISO rating), the more combinations of aperture sizes and shutter speeds the camera can use. Slow film requires a wide aperture, and limits the choice of shutter speed.

The effects of the aperture and shutter speed

Although a correct exposure can be achieved from various combinations of apertures and shutter speeds, each combination produces a slightly different result. The size of the aperture affects the depth-of-field (see below). The choice of shutter speed will determine how a moving subject will appear on the image (either blurred or sharp). With most models, the camera sets a fast enough shutter speed to prevent camera shake, and then selects the aperture.

Apertures and depth-of-field

Depth-of-field is a term used to describe how much of the scene is sharp in front and behind the point where the lens has focused. Some photographs display a very deep depth-of-field, with everything in the foreground and background appearing sharp. Other pictures have very shallow depth-of-field, where the main subject is sharp, but everything in front and behind appears blurred.

This is controlled by the aperture setting. A wide aperture, such as f/2.8,

produces a very shallow depth-of-field, while a small aperture, for example f/16, results in a deep depth-of-field.

Shutter speeds and subject movement

With pictures of static subjects, such as landscapes, you are unlikely to see the effect of using different shutter speeds. However, if there are any moving objects in the frame, this changes. Shutter speeds affect how movement appears in a shot. A slow shutter speed and a fast-moving subject will result in the subject being recorded as a blur, as the action will be captured during exposure. With moving subjects, a fast shutter speed is needed to capture a precise moment in time, and freeze the movement.

Shutter systems

There are different types of shutter used in compact and digital cameras.

Compact cameras

Compacts use two main types of shutter system, the 'between-lens' shutter and the 'focal-plane blind' shutter.

The between-lens shutter is the most common type, and involves the aperture iris doubling as a shutter. Take a photo and the iris opens to the correct aperture setting, and for the relevant amount of time, before closing again. It is a very simple system that is used in all but a handful of compacts.

The focal-plane shutter is a more complex system, and is found in the small number of compacts that feature

interchangeable lenses, such as the Hasselblad Xpan and the Contax G2. The shutter is found in the camera body between the lens and the film and allows lenses to be changed without fogging the film.

Digital cameras

The shutter systems used in compact cameras are not usually necessary in digital cameras, as the exposure is electronically controlled. When the shutter release button is pressed, an electrical charge activates the CCD chip for the necessary amount of time to produce an exposure.

The shutter speed to use is determined by the speed and direction of the subject. A subject moving slowly towards or away from the camera requires a slower shutter speed to freeze it than one moving across the frame, or at speed.

Controlling apertures and shutter speeds

Leave the camera to set the exposure automatically and it will usually produce a good picture. However, as you gain more experience, you'll probably want to have a little more control over the process.

A few compact and digital cameras offer aperture-priority, an exposure mode that allows you to select whatever aperture you wish. This means you can select a wide aperture if you want shallow depth-of-field or a fast shutter speed, or set a narrow aperture for plenty of depth-of-field or a slow shutter speed.

Another way of tailoring the effect is through your choice of film speed. If you want a shallow depth-of-field, use a slow film, because in most situations the camera will select a wide aperture. If you're planning to take some action shots, use a fast film, and the camera will use a faster shutter speed.

Unfortunately, this latter method can be unreliable, because once you load the film, you have no control over the conditions you will encounter. However,

it is easy to change films with APS cameras and is worth a try.

DEPTH-OF-FIELD

As well as the aperture setting, there are other factors that will determine the depth-of-field:

Focal length of the lens

The wider the angle of the lens, the more depth-of-field it produces compared to a longer focal length. For instance, taking a picture with a 35mm lens at f/5.6 will produce greater depth-of-field than taking the shot with a 90mm lens at f/5.6.

⊃ This photograph illustrates the relationship between shutter speeds and subject movement. The foreground is filled with the blurred image of a group of cyclists racing across the frame. The blur is not the result of poor focusing, but rather the speed the cyclists were travelling at. The people in the background have not moved during the exposure and are not blurred.

Subject-to-camera distance

The closer you are to the subject, the less depth-of-field there is. Moving further away increases the depth-of-field.

For maximum depth-of-field, use:

1. A small aperture, such as f/16 or f/22
2. A wide-angle lens, such as 28mm or 35mm
3. A greater distance between the subject and the camera.

For minimum depth-of-field, use:

1. A wide aperture, such as f/2.8 or f/3.5
2. A telephoto lens, such as 100mm
3. A shorter distance between the subject and the camera. ■

Q&A: Apertures and shutter speeds

What does a fast aperture mean?

Some lenses have a wider maximum aperture than is normal for that type of lens. Because the lens allows more light through at its maximum aperture, the shutter speed is faster.

Why does the lens on some zoom compacts have two aperture values?

The maximum aperture of zoom lenses narrows as the focal length extends from the widest angle of the lens to the telephoto setting. The aperture values relate to the maximum aperture of the lens through the zoom. For instance, a 38mm–90mm f/4–f/8 zoom has a maximum aperture of f/4 at 38mm. However, as the zoom extends, the maximum aperture narrows to f/8.

What is the difference between 'small' and 'large' apertures?

A small aperture means the iris has closed up, as when you are taking photographs in bright light, for example. A large aperture means the iris is open for taking pictures in lower light. Confusingly, small apertures have high numbers, such as f/22, while large apertures have low numbers, such as f/2.8.

Is the amount of depth-of-field the same in front of the point of focus as it is behind?

No. There is less depth-of-field in front than behind.

Film

There is a film to suit every imaginable situation, so it is important to choose the right one in order to get the most from your pictures. This section covers all the major types of film available and suggests which are the best for particular occasions and cameras.

You should begin by deciding whether you want to use colour or black-and-white film, and whether you would prefer to have prints or slides. Another consideration should be what film speed will be most suitable for the shots you will be taking. Bear in mind, however, that most compacts feature a mid-roll rewind button that allows you to change films even if you haven't finished the current roll, so you can easily change from one type of film to another.

FILM SPEEDS

Pick up any roll of film and you will see that it has an ISO (International Standards Organisation) number, such as 100, 200 or 400. This refers to the film speed, and is a way of quantifying a film's sensitivity to light. The higher the number, the more sensitive the film. For instance, ISO 400 is twice as sensitive to light as ISO 200, which in turn is twice as sensitive as ISO 100 film. Films with an ISO below 100 are referred to as slow,

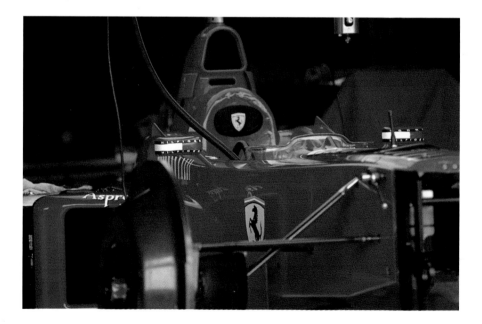

those between ISO 100 and 200 are medium and those with an ISO number of 400 or more are fast-speed films.

There are many factors determining the film's sensitivity to light, but the main one is the size of the film's grain. It is the grain that ultimately forms the photographic image. Large grain is more likely to be hit by light during an exposure than smaller grain, thus fast-speed films use larger grain than slow-speed films.

The size of the grain affects the sharpness of the film, with finer grain resulting in sharper results. So the general rule is that slower films produce sharper images than faster films. With colour films, it is also true to say that the slower the film, the better the colours.

○ Medium-speed films offer good colours and fine grain, making them a perfect choice for general use, such as holiday photos.

○ For saturated colours and excellent sharpness, there is nothing to beat a slow film. This shot of a Formula One Ferrari, taken in dim lighting, still exhibits deep reds.

So why use fast films if they are inferior? Well, film technology has progressed at a substantial rate, resulting in current ISO 400 films that match, or even better, the quality of the ISO 100 films of a decade ago. So fast films can now produce very high-quality images, although slower films will always have the edge in terms of sharpness.

WHAT FILM SPEED SHOULD YOU USE?

Each speed has its own advantages, so choose the one that is most suitable for your camera and subject.

Slow (ISO 25–64)

This type of film offers the highest quality images with superb sharpness and almost invisible grain, but it is only really suitable for the most sophisticated compacts. The film needs very accurate exposure, but most compacts do not offer the range of shutter speeds and apertures to fulfil this requirement. Unless you use top-of-the-range models, such as Contax or Leica, you are better off using ISO 100 film.

Medium (ISO 100–200)

This is the most popular speed of film, combining fine grain with excellent sharpness. Colour films at this speed have excellent colour reproduction, while black-and-white films exhibit a smooth tonal range.

Medium-speed film is useful in all conditions, but is put to the best use in bright situations. The speed is suitable for all types of compacts, but is ideal for fixed-lens models with relatively fast aperture lenses.

⌁ If you're using a zoom compact and conditions are overcast, as they are in this photograph of children playing, an ISO 400 film is recommended to prevent camera shake.

⌁ A fast film is ideal in very low light. If the flash had fired, this photograph would have been washed out. Using a fast film has allowed the subtle colours of the shark to be recorded accurately.

Fast (ISO 400)

Fast films are becoming increasingly popular, thanks to the growing number of zoom compacts on the market. The fast film speed compensates for the relatively slow apertures of the zoom lenses, helping to reduce camera shake and the number of shots requiring flash.

ISO 400 films can be described as the best all-purpose choice, able to handle both bright and overcast conditions.

Very fast (ISO 800+)

Recent improvements in film emulsion have meant that ISO 800 films are becoming increasingly popular. The quality is better than you would traditionally expect from a film of this speed, with prints showing relatively fine grain and good colour reproduction. These films are used for taking handheld photographs in low light. They are a popular choice for sports photography

requiring the fastest possible shutter speeds, and they are also becoming common in single-use cameras. ISO 800 films are a good choice for zoom compacts with powerful telephoto lenses and very small maximum apertures. They are also suitable for taking photographs where flash photography isn't permitted.

Exposure latitude

Exposure latitude is a term that refers to how well a film can cope with the wrong exposure. Colour negative films (see opposite) are able to handle over- and underexposure extremely well, so even if the camera's meter has miscalculated, you should still get a good quality image. Slide films are not as tolerant, so even small errors will tend to result in unsalvageable pictures.

COLOUR NEGATIVE FILM

Often known as print film, this is by far the most popular type, and accounts for the majority of film sales. Images are formed on the film as a negative: dark colours are recorded as light tones, while white appears opaque. When the pictures are printed onto paper, the colours reverse and appear correctly.

Print films offer excellent colours and fine grain, and are able to handle over- and underexposure extremely well, due to their very wide exposure latitude (see panel opposite).

35mm print film
Agfa

HDC PLUS Available in ISO 100, 200 and 400 speeds, this is Agfa's range of print film for the amateur photographer. It produces punchy colours that make it well suited to shooting in overcast conditions. However, the colours are warm so it is not the best choice for portrait photography.

OPTIMA II PRESTIGE Aimed at the professional market, this offers good colour saturation and finer grain than the HDC Plus range of film. However, it is more expensive. It is available in ISO 100, 200 and 400 speeds.

Fuji

SUPERIA This is one of the leading ranges of print film and deserves its success. All the films offer very fine grain and excellent sharpness at their relative speeds. Colour reproduction is on the punchy side and prints show more contrast than the Kodak Gold range.

Two films in this series that deserve a special mention are:

SUPERIA REALA An ISO 100 film that produces extremely realistic colours, making it an ideal choice for portrait work, because skin tones are accurately reproduced. It also boasts extremely fine grain and is one of the sharpest films at this speed. The film has an extra layer, which allows it to reproduce colour in artificial light correctly.

SUPERIA 800 This is the fastest film in the series and there is little difference between it and ISO 400 films. The grain is slightly more noticeable than in slower speed films, but sharpness is good and colours are well recorded.

Kodak

THE GOLD RANGE Available in ISO 100, 200, 400 (Gold Ultra) and ISO 800 (Gold Zoom). The 100 and 200 films are characterized by very fine grain and accurate colours. Gold Ultra and Zoom exhibit very fine grain for their relative speeds, but colours lack some of the punch of other brands.

ROYAL GOLD Kodak's premium amateur range of colour print film is based on the old Ektar series of films. It offers slightly finer grain than the Gold range and much brighter colours.

The ISO 25 emulsion is the slowest print film on the market and can't be bettered for sharpness. However, it isn't designed for compact cameras, so stick with one of the faster films which are all excellent and well worth trying out. The fastest film in the range, Royal Gold 1000, is a fair performer but can't match the sharpness and colour reproduction of ISO 800 films. Also worth considering is the Portra range of ISO 160 and 400 films. Two versions of each speed are available, NC (Natural Colour) and VC (Vibrant Colour). Both offer extremely fine grain and gorgeous skin tones, making them suitable for portraiture.

Konica

THE CENTURIA RANGE This updates Konica's VX emulsions and offers several improvements over the older films. The grain is finer, producing sharper results and colours that are bright and punchy. It is a serious rival to the Fuji and Kodak films and is well worth trying out. Available in ISO 100, 200, 400 and 800. **IMPRESA** This film, available in ISO 100 and 200, produces much subtler tones than the Centuria range. Skin tones are accurate but the muted colours aren't to everyone's taste.

Colour temperature

Colour films are formulated to produce natural colours in daylight. Take pictures in artificial lighting and the photographs will show a strong colour cast. This is because most types of artificial lighting have a different colour temperature to daylight. Tungsten lighting produces a warm, orange cast, while fluorescent lighting results in a pale green cast. For indoor photography, use a flash, which has the same colour temperature as daylight, to prevent these colour casts.

APS print film
Agfa

FUTURA The Futura range is available in ISO 100, 200 and 400 speeds. It is characterized by very punchy colours, but grain size is larger than its competitors, which can be a drawback. This is especially noticeable with the ISO 400 speed where grain is very apparent.

Fuji

NEXIA There were originally two ISO 100 films in the Fuji range: D100 Daylight and F100 Fine-grain. However, only the F100 emulsion is now available. This is an exellent film which offers the finest grain of any APS emulsion and superb sharpness. Fuji Nexia is also available in ISO 200 (A200 All-round) and ISO 400 (H400 Hi-speed).

Kodak

ADVANTIX The Advantix range is made up of ISO 100, 200 and 400 films. All are excellent performers, but perhaps not quite as good as the Fuji films in terms of grain size and sharpness. However, colour reproduction on the Kodak films are more neutral, making them the better choice for realistic colours, compared to Fuji's bolder results. This makes the Kodak films a good choice if you're planning to take portraits and require accurate skin tones.

Konica

JX The JX range is available in ISO 200 and 400 speeds and produces very neutral colours. Although grain isn't as fine as the Fuji or Kodak emulsions, it's not as coarse as the Agfa films.

COLOUR SLIDE FILM

For the ultimate in image quality, nothing compares to slide film. It has finer grain, better sharpness and greater colour saturation than print films, making it the film choice of enthusiasts and professionals. However, it has extremely narrow exposure latitude, so it is critical to get the exposure right. The exposure system of cheap compact cameras isn't sophisticated enough to cope with slide film, but if you've bought a good quality camera, try some out – you're bound to be impressed with the results.

35mm slide film
Agfa

CT Precisa This range of amateur films has bright colours and good sharpness. However, colours aren't as bold as the Fuji films, or as accurate as Kodak's. Available in ISO 100 and 200.

RSX II Agfa's professional film exhibits very fine grain, high sharpness and excellent colour saturation. It's more expensive than many of its rivals but produces excellent results. Available in ISO 100 and 200.

Fuji

Sensia II This is one of the most popular ranges of slide films, offering gorgeous colours, very fine grain and a competitive price. It is available in ISO 100, 200 and 400.

Provia Available in ISO 100, 400 and 1600 speeds, this is the professional version of Sensia and has a similarly high reputation. Colours are accurately reproduced and boast excellent saturation that helps lift images shot in dull conditions. In low light, try out Provia 1600, which offers good colours and reasonably fine grain for the speed.

Velvia and Astia Velvia is an ISO 50 film which produces extremely vivid results, but its very narrow exposure latitude makes it suitable for top-of-the-range compacts only. Astia is an ISO 100 film offering incredibly realistic colours and is an excellent choice for portraits and landscapes.

Kodak

Kodachrome Although Kodachrome has been around for years, it still has plenty to offer. It comes in ISO 25, 64 and 200, although only the ISO 200 speed is recommended for use in compacts. It offers good sharpness but the colours are a little muted compared to rival films. Kodachrome film must be sent to specific Kodak laboratories for processing, so you'll need to wait a few days before you can see the results.

EliteChrome These are excellent amateur films offering accurate colours and very fine grain. If you prefer your colours to look natural then you might find EliteChrome to your taste. It is available in ISO 100, 200 and 400.

APS slide film
Fuji

Nexia 100ix Currently the only APS slide film on the market, Nexia 100ix is based on the emulsion used in the 35mm Provia film. It gives extremely good quality results with excellent colours and sharpness. It takes around two weeks for the film to be processed and the slides are returned mounted in the HDTV format.

BLACK-AND-WHITE FILM

The world is full of colour, but sometimes it looks better photographed in monochrome. Black-and-white film has a graphic simplicity that lends itself to a variety of subjects, from striking portraits and atmospheric landscapes to documentary photography (see pages 120–125). Black-and-white film is available in a wide range of speeds, so there is no excuse not to give it a try.

⊙ Black-and-white photos can have a timeless quality. Often a scene, such as this canal shot, looks better in black and white than colour, so always keep a roll or two handy.

Black-and-white tonal range

Black-and-white films record colours as a range of greys, varying from solid blacks to clean whites. This series of greys is referred to as the tonal range.

35mm black-and-white film
Agfa
AGFAPAN APX This is characterized by fine grain and high sharpness. The ISO 25 speed isn't recommended for compacts, but the ISO 100 and 400 speeds produce excellent results.

Ilford
THE DELTA RANGE Available in ISO 100, 400 and 3200, this has almost everything you could want from a black-and-white film, boasting excellent sharpness and relatively fine grain.
XP2 SUPER This is probably the best starter film available. It is an ISO 400 film offering superb sharpness, extremely fine

grain and a great range of tones. The most important feature of the XP2 Super is its chromogenic emulsion (see Q&A panel), which allows for developing in standard (C-41) colour processing.

Fuji

NEOPAN These films combine excellent sharpness and a good tonal range. Both speeds (ISO 400 and 1600) exhibit very fine grain but the high speed ISO 1600 is the most impressive.

Kodak

THE T-MAX RANGE These films (ISO 100, 400 and 3200) produce excellent results but must be processed in the T-Max developer for the best effect. The ISO 400 film is one of the best in its class, with very fine grain and excellent sharpness. The huge grain size of T-Max 3200 makes it suitable for moody images. T-Max T400CN offers excellent sharpness and fine grain, and can be put through colour processing units.

APS black-and-white film
Kodak

ADVANTIX BLACK AND WHITE Advantix is a chromogenic film based on T-Max T400CN and produces very similar results to the 35mm version, although it is not as sharp.

Black-and-white slide film
Agfa

SCALA 200X This is a very high-quality ISO 200 film, with fine grain and high sharpness. However, it can be processed only by certain specialist labs or through mail-order companies. ∎

Q&A: Film

What is chromogenic film?

Unlike conventional film, chromogenic film uses dyes rather than silver to form the image. This results in very fine grain and a wide exposure latitude. There is also a clear advantage to using a black-and-white chromogenic film that can be processed using colour chemistry. You can simply take it to your local lab where processing is faster and cheaper than for standard black-and-white films.

What is a reversal film?

This is another term to describe a slide film, which can also be called a tranny or transparency.

What do the codes C-41 and E-6 on the film box mean?

They are the standard processing procedures for print film and slide film respectively.

I've taken some indoor pictures without flash and they have an orange cast. Why?

Tungsten lighting has a warmer colour temperature than sunlight. Almost all colour films are balanced for daylight, which means that pictures taken in tungsten light appear to have an orange cast.

How should film be handled?

Film can be adversely affected by temperature and humidity. Store in a dark, cool environment and process promptly once used.

Buying a camera

With the enormous number of cameras on the market, deciding which one to choose can seem bewildering and buying the wrong type of compact or digital camera can be a costly mistake. The following advice will help you to decide which is the best model for you.

COMPACT CAMERAS
What type should I buy?
As a general rule, it is always worth buying the best camera you can afford. More money will buy more features, and a better quality lens. At the very least, aim to buy a fixed-lens autofocus model. This will offer all the basic features as well as a decent quality wide-angle lens.

If you are prepared to invest a little more, you could buy a camera with a limited (though useful) zoom range of around 38–80mm. This will provide greater versatility for general picture-taking and, usually, a few more features.

The next spending bracket will buy you a zoom compact with more impressive zoom ranges (usually around 38–115mm or 38–145mm) and fixed-lens compacts with very high-quality lenses. The extra power of the zoom lens gives you more scope for practising creative techniques, as well as bringing distant subjects closer.

Finally, there's the premium range of compacts, usually featuring extremely high-quality interchangeable lenses.

Essential features
We have already looked at the general features of most compacts, but which are the really important ones, and which are the ones you can do without?

Having an autofocus lens is essential, as this is the first step to taking sharp pictures. Avoid those with a fixed-focus lens, as the image quality can be poor. A zoom-lens compact has become the most popular choice, as it makes composing a picture much easier than having to physically move backward and forward.

An integral flash is usually standard, but you should check to see how many flash modes the camera has. Fill-in flash, flash-off override and red-eye reduction are all features that can play an important role in improving your picture-taking.

Built-in autowinders to move the film on are found on virtually all compacts, and take the trouble out of winding on between pictures and rewinding the film when it's finished. Some models offer a continuous shooting mode, frame after frame being taken when you hold the shutter release button down, which is a useful feature for action photography.

These are the main features but there are a few additional facilities worth considering. These include a spot meter for producing correct exposures in difficult lighting conditions, and a Bulb facility, which allows you to make extremely long exposures (useful for night photography). Many compacts are also weather-resistant, making them ideal when you are photographing in bad weather, or on seaside or skiing holidays. Finally, camera outfits are well worth considering, particularly for the beginner.

Film formats: 35mm or APS?

35mm film has been the most popular choice for decades, but APS has now become a major competitor.

Traditionally, the main advantage of 35mm was the wide range of films on the market. Colour print, colour slide, black-and-white print and slide film, as well as special films such as infrared, are all on offer in 35mm. Until recently, only colour print film was available in APS, but now black-and-white film and colour slide have arrived in this format.

We have already looked in detail at the advantages of APS (see pages 22–27), but in short, the film cartridges are smaller, easier to load, have a choice of print formats and include a date-printing facility as standard.

Although many APS cameras are smaller than 35mm ones, the difference isn't always obvious. Some 35mm compacts, such as the Olympus Mju II, compare favourably with their APS rivals for size. It is worth noting that small cameras can present their own problems, such as being difficult to grip if you have large hands, or covering the flash accidentally with your fingers.

Ultimately, you need to decide what is most important to you. It is likely you will find the look and feel of a particular compact more important than the type of film it uses, which is not necessarily a bad thing; if you're comfortable with the camera you're more likely to use it.

↻ A selection of 35mm and APS film

The kit usually contains a few free accessories such as a case, some film and a mini photo album.

DIGITAL CAMERAS
What type should I buy?

Before rushing out to buy the latest model, you should work out what your requirements are. If you intend only to put pictures onto your computer and not print them out, then any of the low- to medium-resolution cameras will be suitable. However, if you want to produce good quality pictures then you should consider a megapixel camera. The basic rule is that the more pixels the camera has, the better the results. Again, buy the best you can afford.

Essential features

As with compact cameras, digital cameras come with either fixed-focus or autofocus lenses. You should avoid the fixed-focus type if you want to produce pictures with acceptable sharpness.

There are plenty of models on the market featuring a fixed wide-angle lens, but if you want a high degree of flexibility, choose one with a zoom lens.

Image storage is another important consideration. Opt for a camera with removable memory cards, as this allows

The pros and cons

If you are still confused about which type of compact to buy, use this checklist to assess the main strengths and weaknesses of each format.

35mm cameras

Pros

- Highest quality images
- 35mm is an established film standard
- Hundreds of models on the market, from cheap and fun disposables to professional models

Cons

- Cameras can be large and bulky
- Loose negatives can be easily lost or damaged
- Film loading problems

APS cameras

Pros

- Cameras are very small
- New index print
- Negatives stay safely in film canister
- Three print formats
- Information exchange improves print quality

Cons

- Quality not as good as 35mm film
- Film and processing costs more expensive than 35mm

Digital cameras

Pros

- Instant images, so no negatives to lose
- No film or processing costs
- You can transfer images to your PC for use in e-mail or on the Internet

Cons

- Lowest quality images of all three formats
- Most require connection to a computer to produce prints

you to take many more pictures than a camera that uses only its internal memory to store images.

A model that features an LCD monitor and an optical viewfinder is also worth considering because the latter can be used to compose a picture without using up battery power.

Several digital cameras offer excellent close-up facilities, so if you intend to use your camera for this purpose, make sure the one you choose has this feature.

Finally, make sure the camera is compatible with your computer. Most cameras come supplied with software that will allow them to work with IBM PC and Apple Macintosh computers, but some work with one computer system only, so it's worth checking before you purchase your camera.

WHERE SHOULD I BUY MY CAMERA?

The high-street chains have the advantage of accessibility, so if something goes wrong with the camera, it is easy to return it to your local branch. However, because these stores handle an enormous number of products, it is sometimes difficult to find a member of staff who can answer in-depth questions about the cameras. Specialist camera shops are the place to go for expert advice, but they usually keep a smaller range of cameras in stock. Mail order is a convenient option, enabling you to order products over the telephone. However, it does mean that you have to wait at least a couple of days for your purchase to arrive and it can be more difficult to obtain after-sales service, should something go wrong with the equipment. ■

Guarantees, warranties and finance schemes

It's always worth checking what type of guarantee your camera has. Most cameras come with a one-year guarantee, but some manufacturers offer a two- or even a five-year guarantee. Some manufacturers supply a worldwide guarantee, while others will guarantee the camera only in the country of purchase.

Some retailers offer extended warranties, at extra cost, that cover the camera from defect for a further three to five years and may offer insurance cover for accidental damage, loss and theft. It is debatable whether or not these extended warranties are worth having, as cameras are built to very high standards and will usually give reliable service for several years.

As well as simply using a credit card, there are many finance schemes available that make buying a camera much easier. Some schemes do not charge interest and spread payments over a long period of time, while others charge a set rate of interest. Clearly, the former is preferable, but you will have to pay a deposit (usually 10 per cent of the total value) and repay the rest in monthly instalments. 'Buy now, pay later' schemes are another option.

Care and maintenance

Many photographs are ruined simply because the photographer mishandles the camera while taking the pictures or stores the camera incorrectly. But if you know how to look after your camera properly, it should reward you with years of trouble-free use.

LOOKING AFTER YOUR CAMERA

Following these do's and don'ts will help ensure that your camera stays in top condition.

DON'T: Get your camera wet.
Do: Make sure it doesn't come into contact with water, which is obviously a major hazard to any electrical device (unless it's water-resistant or waterproof). Never load film in wet conditions, as water can get into the camera. If your camera does get wet, wipe it thoroughly with a dry cloth.

DON'T: Store your camera on a windowsill.
Do: Keep the camera out of direct sunlight, as this can cause it to overheat. Condensation can also be damaging, so protect the camera from humidity. Store your camera in a cool, dry place.

DON'T: Leave a partly used film in the camera.
Do: Process films promptly, as the pictures taken on an unprocessed film degrade over a period of time.

DON'T: Leave the battery loaded in the camera for lengthy periods.
Do: Remove the battery if you're not planning to use the camera for a long period of time. Leaving alkaline batteries in the camera runs the risk of battery acid leakage, which will corrode the camera's internal parts. Lithium batteries are safer, but manufacturers still recommend that you remove them.

DON'T: Walk around holding the camera loosely in your hand.
Do: Keep a strap attached to the camera. A neck strap allows you to hang the camera from your neck, leaving both hands free. Alternatively, invest in a wrist strap. Keep the camera protected in a case when not in use.

DON'T: Clean your camera lens with an item of clothing.
Do: Use a lens cleaning cloth for wiping the lens surface. The soft fibre of these specialist cloths will wipe off dust and dirt without scratching the optics.

DON'T: Leave the camera unused for long periods.
Do: Use the camera briefly every couple of weeks to make sure it is in perfect working order.

DON'T: Leave your camera on the beach unprotected.
Do: Keep the camera in a protective case when it is not in use. This will prevent sand and sea spray from getting inside and causing damage.

HOW TO HOLD YOUR CAMERA

Handling your camera correctly when taking a picture can make a significant difference to your photography.

DON'T: Obstruct the flash with your fingers.

Do: Make sure you are not covering the flashgun with your finger, otherwise your subject will not be lit properly. This can be a particular problem with very small compacts, as the left hand can easily cover the flash. Some cameras, such as the Fuji Fotonex 250ix, have a warning light that flashes in the viewfinder if a finger strays over a sensor around the flashgun.

DON'T: Obstruct your lens.

Do: Remember that a clear view through the viewfinder window doesn't mean that the lens isn't obstructed. If you are holding the camera in its upright position, make sure that the camera strap isn't dangling in front of the lens. Avoiding this problem is simple – keep the strap wrapped around your wrist. You will also need to take care if you have long hair, as it can easily fall in front of the lens and ruin a shot. ∎

Avoiding camera shake

Holding your camera correctly and adopting the right stance helps to eliminate camera shake and improves your photography:

- Hold the camera in both hands with the left hand supporting the bottom corner of the camera.
- Stand with your legs slightly apart, keep your back straight and tuck your elbows in to provide balanced support. Crouching down on one knee also provides a stable shooting position.
- Lean against a wall for extra support.
- Hold your breath when you are about to press the shutter release button.

Film processing

The days when only your local chemist could handle your film are long gone. Processing, or 'D&P' (developing and printing) as it is also known, is now widely available. There are labs on just about every high street or you can send your print films off to a mail-order firm.

Prices vary from place to place, but the majority of processors offer some, or all, of the following services.

One-hour processing
Drop your film off and your prints are ready for collection an hour later. This is usually the most expensive service but is very useful if you need your pictures in a hurry.

Three- or four-hour processing
If you're not so desperate to see your pictures, this is a good option. The turnaround time is convenient, as you can drop the film off in the morning and collect it in your lunch hour, or hand it in during lunch and collect it after work.

24-hour processing
This is usually the cheapest way of having your pictures developed in the high street.

Print sizes
The usual size for prints is 6x4in. In some places the standard size is 5x3½in, while other processors offer a 7x5in print at no extra cost. Check the print size before you hand your film in, as the pictures may not fit your photo albums.

The films are usually collected early in the morning and returned late in the afternoon.

Mail-order processing
You usually have to wait about a week for your pictures to be returned. Some mail-order companies supply a free film with your pictures to entice you to keep using their service.

Reprints
Many people often wait until they have their film processed and returned before deciding what reprints they require. This works well if you plan to have only one or two pictures reprinted. However, if you know in advance that you will need several reprints – of wedding photos, for example – ask for an extra set of reprints when you hand the film in. The cost of having a complete extra set is often the same as for only four or five reprints at a later date.

Slide films
These can take three to seven days to be processed. You can usually stipulate whether you want them returned mounted or unmounted. ■

Taking your photos further

Most people do little more with their pictures than
have reprints and enlargements made for their
friends and family. Below are some alternative ideas
for utilizing your favourite pictures. Most of these
services are provided by high-street processors,
while others are available only through mail order.

Calendars

Many high-street processors can now print your
pictures onto your own calendar. There are usually
several options available, from having one to three
pictures per month, to a single picture for one, three
or six months.

Canvas prints

If you want your photograph to have a classic
appearance, have it printed onto canvas and framed.
This is becoming increasingly popular and is a good
way of giving the image a timeless feel.

Photo CD-ROMs

An increasingly popular service is having all your
pictures supplied on a CD-ROM. The disk comes with
your usual prints and means you can easily access
your pictures on a computer and e-mail them to
friends or relatives anywhere in the world.

T-shirts and jigsaws

Wear your picture with pride by
having it put onto a T-shirt. You can
usually have the image placed on
the front or back of the T-shirt and
also have a message printed around
it. Or you can give your kids a treat
by turning one of their favourite
pictures into a jigsaw puzzle.

Accessories

You can supplement your essential photographic equipment with a variety of accessories, from devices to help you take better pictures, such as tripods, to projectors for showing off the results. Most are affordable and readily available.

CAMERA CARE

Having invested in a new camera, it's wise to spend just a little more and buy an accessory or two to keep it in good working order for years to come.

Camera case

Not all compacts come supplied with a case and if yours doesn't, make it the first accessory you buy. A case has two main functions – protection and convenience.

A case protects your camera from the elements, so you don't have to worry about it getting damaged if you're caught in the rain. A case also guards against damage should you drop your camera, and prevents unsightly scratches or scuff marks from appearing. Most cases have a belt attachment, so you can carry the camera while keeping your hands free. Some also have an additional pocket for storing extra rolls of film. Cases come in all shapes, sizes and colours but a padded pouch is the best option, as it can absorb greater impact.

Lens cleaning cloth

Have you ever noticed marks on your camera's lens and then cleaned it with the end of your shirt or blouse? If the answer is 'yes', hang your head in shame.

Although lenses are coated with protective layers to protect them from damage, some materials are too abrasive and can scratch the exposed optics. A lens cleaning cloth, made from either soft chamois or microfibre, is specifically designed to wipe dirt and fingerprints from delicate surfaces. You should always wipe the lens gently from the centre to the edge.

Silica gel

Moisture can seriously damage your camera, but can be easily avoided. Invest in some sachets of silica gel and always keep one inside the camera case. Silica gel is a chemical which absorbs water and is available from most major photographic outlets. The sachet needs replacing every few weeks.

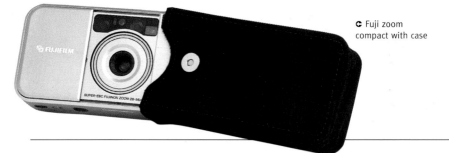

c Fuji zoom compact with case

accessories

GENERAL ACCESSORIES
Tripods

Compact cameras are designed for portability so you might think that a tripod isn't necessary. However, don't totally dismiss the idea, as there are occasions when a tripod will come in very useful. Also, if you think that tripods are large and heavy, you will be surprised to find that some can actually fit inside a pocket or handbag. The following are all suitable for compact cameras.

TABLE-TOP TRIPOD This costs little more than a couple of rolls of film and is a good investment. The tripod stands little more than a few inches tall, but is useful when you want to take a picture of yourself and can't find a flat surface on which to rest the camera. Its small size means it is very sturdy, so you don't have to worry about the camera toppling over. Some have flexible legs that allow you to position the camera at the required angle. Table-top tripods fold up flat when not in use, so they take up very little space and are extremely portable.

MINI TRIPOD This is a little larger than the table-top variety and although it is less easy to carry around, it offers a couple of extra features. The main addition is a movable head which allows you to point the camera in the direction you want. The sturdier legs can often be extended to increase the camera height, so a mini tripod tends to be more suitable for the larger sized compacts than a table-top tripod.

TRIPOD The standard tripod is the best option if you want to take a picture at eye-level and need some form of support. A fairly lightweight model is suitable for a compact camera, but you should ensure that it is not so light as to lack stability. Check that when fully extended, the tripod won't topple over if nudged.

MONOPOD As the name suggests, a monopod has only one leg, making it far more portable than a standard tripod and the ideal choice for long treks. You need to hold the monopod at all times, so although it's not suitable for self-timer shots, it's useful if you're taking a photograph in low light and know that hand-holding the camera will result in camera shake.

Ω Table-top tripod

73

Hand-held reflector

If you're keen on portraiture, a small, portable reflector is a worthwhile investment. Positioned just out of the frame, it is useful for reflecting light onto the subject's face and eliminating shadows under the chin, eyes and nose.

There are many types to choose from, but the collapsible reflector is probably the best as it is easy to store away and opens up to a good working size. Most reflectors have a white or silver surface, but gold versions are available tò add a warm hue to the light.

Film retriever

This little device allows you to recover the leader from a 35mm cassette if it has completely rewound inside. It is useful if you want to reload a partly used film, or plan to take multiple exposures.

Underwater housing

Don't limit your photography to land. If you want to take full advantage of your compact while on holiday, why not use your camera underwater? There are many types of housing available that will allow you to use the camera under the waves, usually to a depth of about five metres. The housings are little more than watertight transparent plastic bags, albeit made from very tough material. Even if you're not planning to go diving or snorkelling, a housing is still worth considering if you want to use the camera on a beach. It will protect the camera from sand, which can cause problems with the film transport system, and from the corrosive salt found in sea-spray.

DX-coded stickers

If your camera does not allow you to override its DX-coding (see page 16), there is a way to trick it into doing so. Stickers imprinted with DX-codes can be attached to the film cassette, allowing you to use the film at the speed of your

Filters

For black-and-white film

Filter	Effect
Red	Darkens sky considerably, but lightens red and orange subjects. Reduces haze.
Orange	Produces moderate darkening of sky. Slightly reduces haze.
Green	Lightens foliage.

For colour film

Filter	Effect
Polarizer	Produces saturated blue skies and reduces reflections.
Ultra-violet (UV)	Reduces haze. Protects lens from damage.
Red	Use with Kodak colour infrared film.

choice. This is very useful if you want to try out a technique such as cross processing (see pages 180–181).

Filters

A few compacts accept filters that attach to the front of the lens, opening up new possibilities for creative picture-taking. Filters can be used with colour or black-and-white films, and allow you to experiment with, and enhance, your photography. The main filters are listed in the box on the opposite page.

SLIDE ACCESSORIES

There are better ways to view slides than holding them up to a window! So make the most of your slides with these useful viewing and storing accessories.

SLIDE PROJECTOR We've all had to endure a friend's four-hour holiday slide show, but don't let that put you off buying a projector. A slide projector is one of the best ways to view the fantastic colours and detail that this type of film has to offer. Some projectors include their own screen so you can view images without having to project the image onto a wall. However, these screens are usually not very well made, so if you're serious about your slides, invest in a large projection screen.

LIGHTBOX AND LUPE A lightbox has bulbs inside that give daylight-balanced light and is an essential piece of equipment for checking slides. Use a high quality lupe (eyeglass) for viewing the slides at high magnification.

SLIDE VIEWER This relatively inexpensive accessory allows you to view a magnified image of a slide on its screen.

SLIDE FILING AND SLEEVES Slides are originals, so it is important to look after them by filing and storing them properly in slide sleeves. These transparent sleeves hold an average of 20 slides and can be hung in cabinets or stored in ring-binder folders.

Most sleeves are made from PVC, which is a tough, high-quality plastic. However, if you plan to store your slides for many years to come, use sleeves made from polypropylene, which offer even better protection.

SLIDE TRAYS If you have a large number of slides, you may prefer to store them in a slide tray. These come in various sizes, but most are able to accommodate hundreds of slides.

PRESENTATION

Don't hide your favourite photographs away in a shoebox under the bed! Picture frames are an excellent way to display your images and they are available in a myriad of shapes and sizes, from simple aluminium or wooden frames to ornate silver-plated designs. Another popular type is the clipframe, which uses metal clips to hold a sheet of glass against the background board. You can even buy inflatable frames in a variety of fun shapes and colours.

The important thing is to choose a frame that complements the photograph. Always use mounts and try to avoid hanging glass-fronted frames opposite a window, unless you are using non-reflective glass. Photograph albums, such as flip albums which can hold hundreds of prints, are another good way to display and look after your favourite images. ∎

Chapter Two

TECHNIQUES

Advances in modern technology have meant that photography has never been more popular or accessible, and the arrival of a new generation of user-friendly cameras has helped to take much of the trial and error out of capturing images. However, there is more to taking good pictures than going out and buying the most up-to-date or expensive equipment. Nor is it simply about point-and-shoot. Whether you opt for a 35mm or APS camera or decide to go down the digital route, traditional photographic techniques, such as achieving a good composition, filling the frame, making the most of light and colour, and including focal points, still apply. Focusing on a range of subjects, from people and landscapes to travel and special effects, this chapter will guide you through many of the practical and creative techniques that will enable you to go out and take stunning shots.

Composition

Often, the difference between a good and a great image is the way the different parts of the shot are arranged. A well-composed shot is one that has all the elements in the right balance, resulting in an image that is pleasing to the eye.

THE RULE OF THIRDS

The most common aid to composition is the rule of thirds, which was originally devised by painters but applies equally to photography. It's a very easy principle to pick up and once you get into the habit of using it, you should find that your photographs will look more balanced.

So here's what to do. Imagine the scene divided up by two vertical and horizontal lines to produce nine equally sized rectangles. You should compose the scene so that the object of interest sits at one of the points where the lines intersect. This means that the subject is positioned one third to the left or right of the edge of the frame and one third from the top or bottom of it. So, if you're photographing a landscape and there's a lone tree in the scene, position it where the lines intersect rather than in the centre of the frame. Place the horizon on one of the horizontal thirds rather than along the centre of the frame. With the horizon

↻ Finding a subject with which to lead the eye into the scene wasn't difficult in this shot taken at Arlington cemetery in Washington DC. The lines of gravestones pull the eye toward the centre of the frame where hundreds of other gravestones are visible. A wide-angle lens was used to draw as many rows as possible into view and maximize the impact of the scene. A punchy colour film has made the most of the blue sky.

➲ Look for ways to lead the eye into the frame. In this example, the curve of the wooden musical instrument pulls the eye toward the musician.

↺ This perfectly composed image has been achieved by using the rule of thirds. The ball boy, in sharp focus, has been placed on the left of the frame and is looking into the scene. The net leads the eye into the frame, with the legs of the tennis players appearing out of focus in the background.

positioned along the top third, you will draw attention to the foreground, while placing it along the bottom line will emphasize the sky.

Although the rule of thirds is used extensively in landscape photography, where it helps the viewer to find a focal point in a large expanse of scenery, it can be applied to almost any subject. If you're photographing a head-and-shoulders portrait, for instance, place one of the subject's eyes at an intersection. For full-length body shots, position the subject away from the centre of the frame.

↷ The rule of thirds is as important for a panoramic shot as it is for a standard frame format. Here the bridge extends across the top third while the boat is positioned in the right third of the frame.

Pay attention to detail when composing the scene. For portraits, ensure that there isn't a tree or telegraph pole behind your subject. You should also think about perspective. Altering your position can make a dramatic difference to a shot. Say you're photographing a building. Rather than pointing the camera straight at the subject and shooting from a normal

➲ This very simple composition relies on the colours and form of the subject. The round black ring is set against a straight white stripe which itself contrasts with the deep green water beneath it.

standing position, get closer, crouch down and shoot upward. It's amazing the difference a little thought and a short walk can make.

It is recommended that a moving subject should be travelling toward the centre of the frame rather than away from it. This is because the viewer will unconsciously follow the direction of the subject, and your aim is to have them take a good look at your image rather than to lead their eye away from it.

There is always an exception to every rule, however, and that can be said of the rule of thirds. Sometimes abandoning the rules of composition and placing the subject dead centre in the frame can produce effective results. If you were shooting mountains with a large lake in the foreground, for instance, you could place the horizon along the middle of the frame because the reflection of the mountain in the lake would bring a pleasing symmetry to the scene.

↻ The rule of thirds has been abandoned for this beach shot, which places the horizon across the centre of the frame. A wide-angle lens was used to emphasize the number of identical sun umbrellas and also to fill the frame with the deep blue sky and white sand.

⋒ A derelict bus on a remote hill in Crete provided an unusual subject. Rather than including only the bus in the frame, a tree was also featured to provide scale and to bring a sense of isolation to the scene.

↻ This photograph of a Thai dancer was taken on an APS camera, with the 'H' format selected to include as much of the subject in the frame as possible. Notice how the two key elements in the shot – the dancer's face and the fan – have been carefully positioned according to the rule of thirds.

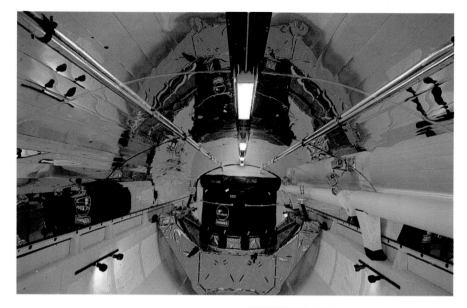

↷ Symmetry is an important aspect of composition. The inside of the cargo bay of the space shuttle Explorer was photographed with the reflections included in the frame. The combination of curves and straight lines works well, and the artificial lighting has produced an unusual mix of colours.

⤵ Look for anything unusual which could make an interesting picture, such as this rollercoaster sculpture dominating a high street in Gothenburg, Sweden. The shot was taken with a wide-angle lens and contrasts the curves of the rollercoaster rails with the straight lines of the red-and-white tape in the foreground.

FOCAL POINTS AND COLOUR

Focal points are elements that help to draw the eye into the frame and they can play a key role in a good composition. A focal point can either be the main centre of interest, as in a portrait or still life, for instance, or it can be a feature, such as a lone tree or farmhouse on a rugged landscape, that helps to give a sense of scale and visual balance.

Colour, too, can be a defining element. A deep blue sky, for instance, or the multi-coloured stripes on the side of a boat may be enough to create a well-composed image. Often the best compositions are those that incorporate two or three vibrant, contrasting colours that grab the viewer's attention. This works especially well when the subjects themselves are not especially inspiring.

PROJECTS

THE RULE OF THIRDS Take four pictures that show good use of the rule of thirds. At least one should be a landscape and another a portrait.

ABANDONING THE RULE OF THIRDS Take two well-composed pictures that do not follow the rule of thirds by positioning the main subject directly in the middle of the frame.

SYMMETRY Look for and photograph two scenes that show good symmetry. One should be a reflection.

COLOUR AND COMPOSITION Take two pictures in which colour plays a major role in the composition. Include a backdrop of blue sky in one of them. ■

Q&A: Composition

Does the rule of thirds apply to upright shots?

Yes. The rule of thirds applies to all pictures regardless of which way you hold the camera.

What subjects produce a strong composition?

A combination of curves and straight lines makes an interesting image. If you are shooting a landscape, look for isolated subjects, such as trees set against a plain backdrop, or something that leads the eye into the picture, such as a fence, a winding river or a road.

What should I do if the subject has a very distracting background?

Try altering your viewpoint by moving to another position or getting closer so the subject fills the frame.

Should the main focal point always be nearest the camera?

Not at all. You will often find that many successful pictures feature the main subject in the distance. What is important is to make sure that the viewer's eye is led into the frame.

How can I keep the main subject sharp if I have to position it off-centre for a well-composed shot?

You will need to use a feature known as the focus lock. By pressing and holding the shutter halfway while the subject is in the centre of the frame, you can lock the focus of the subject, allowing you to recompose the shot.

Contrasting colours

It is normally the subject that dominates a picture, but there are occasions when it is the combination of colours included in the shot that becomes the main focus of attention and provides the essential ingredient to the picture's success.

Strong colours that visually clash are known as contrasting colours and lie opposite each other on the colour wheel (see panel opposite). Vibrant colour combinations, such as reds and greens, compete for the viewer's attention and can be incorporated into your photographs to create bold and dynamic effects. These colours can help to draw attention to the main subject in the photograph or they can make visually arresting patterns in their own right. However, the most effective images are usually those that contain no more than two or three of these contrasting hues, otherwise the effect can be too confusing. Some colours, including reds, yellows and oranges, stand out in pictures, so try to keep these in the foreground, while others such as blues and greens tend to work best in the background.

↻ Making colours rather than the subject the main focus of interest can result in some exciting abstract shots. These ropes were lying side by side on the deck of a yacht. Using the close-up facility has allowed the frame to be filled with colour.

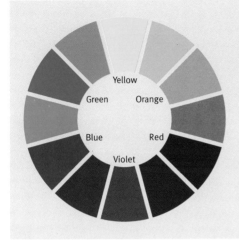

Colour wheel

Understanding how different colours work together can make a significant difference to the way you compose your photographs. This colour wheel is your guide to working out which colours clash and which ones blend. Contrasting or complementary colours, such as red and green or blue and orange, are shown on opposite sides of the wheel. When they are used together they create eye-catching, vibrant effects. Harmonious colours, such as yellow and orange, are adjacent on the wheel.

Inspiration for exciting combinations of colour can be found in many different places, so always keep your eyes peeled. A field of yellow flowers below a deep blue sky or a red car parked in front of a light blue garage door, could both make striking images. Local markets can be another good source of eye-catching contrasts of colour. Even commonplace objects, such as traffic signs or corporate logos, can be commandeered into service. Shoot from a low viewpoint or an unusual angle to create an interesting composition, and try to include a contrasting background.

If you're having trouble finding suitable subjects, you can always set up your own colourful still lifes. This way you can pick and mix the colours of your subjects and therefore maximize the impact of the result. Also, if your camera has a close-up facility, you can isolate small parts of an object to produce a colourful abstract.

Camera
Any type of camera is suitable. If you are planning to set up your own colourful still lifes, a close-up mode will be extremely useful.

Film
For maximum impact, opt for a colour film that produces punchy colours. A slow- to medium-speed film is the best choice for making the most of the strong colours.

Exposure
The time of day you shoot can make a significant difference to the way colours appear. In the early morning, the light is warmer and more diffuse, resulting in a slight orange tint, but by mid-afternoon, when the sun is high in the sky, colours look more vibrant. Shooting in bright sunlight will also mean that you can incorporate the bright blue of the sky into

◯ Bright, sunny days provide the perfect opportunity for capturing some exciting outdoor colours, as can be seen in these two shots. The deep blue sky provided the perfect backdrop for this gold sign (top), while cropping tight on the top of the sign has produced an attractive pattern with bold colours. Shooting on a sunny day has also helped to bring a resonance to the colours of this Stars and Stripes flag (above). The photographer used a zoom to roughly frame the shot and waited until the wind had unfurled the flag.

the frame. When night draws in, a whole new world of colour – in the form of artificial lighting – presents itself. Visit the centre of town and you are bound to find an array of bright neon lights. Remember to take along a tripod and switch the flash off to get the best results.

PROJECTS

The world is full of exciting colour combinations, so aim to include some of them in your photo album.

NEON SIGNS Take four pictures of neon signs showing good contrasting colours. Shoot at night and make sure you use a tripod to keep the camera steady.

OUTDOOR SCENES Find four different scenes which incorporate clearly contrasting colours and photograph them. Two of the pictures should include a deep blue sky as a backdrop. Try to show examples of natural colour contrasts, as well as man-made subjects such as brightly painted doors.

INTERIOR SHOTS Take two pictures inside your home of subjects with contrasting colours. ■

☾ Venturing out into a town or city after dark can result in some eye-catching night-time photographs. Most neon signs use bright colours to catch your attention at night. Mount your compact on a tripod, frame the sign and snap away. The pitch-black night sky makes a fitting backdrop for this vibrant red, yellow and white advertising sign.

Q&A: Contrasting colours

Which subjects are most suitable?
Anything that features two or three strong colours is ideal. Create a vibrant still life with fruit or flowers or look for brightly painted objects such as a yellow car parked in front of a black garage door, or frame road signs against a backdrop of blue sky.

How can I achieve maximum impact with my colours?
For really saturated colours, use a punchy film such as Fuji Sensia II slide film or Agfa HDC Plus print film. If you're taking pictures outdoors, shoot in bright sunlight in mid-afternoon for maximum colour. In overcast conditions, use fill-in flash to add a bit of sparkle to the results.

Are metallic objects suitable?
Silver or gold objects, such as cutlery or coins, combine well with a variety of colours. Silver spoons scooped into powdered paints in a rainbow of shades, for instance, would make a good still-life subject.

I've had some prints returned and the colours aren't as bright and bold as I remember them. Why?
Even if you use colour print film capable of punchy results, it's often the case that the prints are dull in comparison to the actual colours of the subject. This often occurs when you use a low-cost, fast turnaround lab, so It's worth paying a little more for a premium processing service.

Landscapes

It's a beautiful world we live in, so make sure you capture as much of it as possible with your camera. For many people, breathtaking landscapes are only a couple of hours' drive away, so make the effort to wake up early one morning and head for the hills.

Landscapes are one of the most popular subjects for photography and offer a rich source of inspiration for great shots. Being static, they are relatively straightforward to capture, but they can offer a constantly changing pageant of colour, pattern and texture, depending on when you decide to shoot.

The secret to creating great landscape photographs is to take some time to observe the area – at different times of the day and from different vantage points – to get a feel for its changing moods and rhythms. So don't be afraid to venture off the beaten path from time to time and really get to know the place before you begin snapping away.

Weather conditions and seasonal changes can have a significant impact on how a scene looks, so it's always worth returning to the same location at different times of the year. On dark, wet days, for instance, foreboding clouds will help to inject a moody, atmospheric element in your photographs. If you're lucky, a break in the clouds will lead to a bright streak of light piercing the cloud cover. You could even be treated to a rainbow. If so, try to set it against a dark backdrop so that the colours will stand out.

If you're not familiar with the scenic areas around your home town, it's worth visiting a local library or tourist office. Ordnance Survey maps provide an invaluable guide to the topography of the region and will help you to locate landmarks such as hills, rivers, footpaths and roads. Often you will find that the best places to visit are ones with plenty of hills or mountains and those with lakes and rivers. Coastlines, too, offer plenty of scope for stunning shots.

LIGHT

Choosing when to shoot is crucial to capturing great landscapes. Light changes during the course of the day and can have a dramatic effect on how a scene looks. It's important to note the position of the sun when taking pictures outdoors. Try to avoid shooting at midday when the sun is high in the sky, because the light isn't particularly flattering and can make the landscape look flat and uninteresting. Instead, try to shoot early in the morning or late in the afternoon when the light is less harsh and the lower angle of the sun brings out the texture of the landscape.

Wherever possible, shoot with the sun behind you to prevent flare from spoiling your pictures. Flare is the result of stray light reflecting off the glass in the lens, and shows up in the photograph as bright spots of light. If you are shooting into the light, try to keep the sun out of the frame, or try to obstruct it behind an object such as a hill or a tree.

COMPOSITION

The rule of thirds is extremely important in landscape photography (see also pages 78–85). One simple method for improving your composition technique is to place the horizon along the upper or lower third of the picture. If there is plenty of foreground interest, put the horizon along the upper third. If there is good detail in the sky, such as some

☾ The rule of thirds is an important technique for landscape photography. In this shot of Casares in Andalusia, Spain, the horizon has been placed along the top third of the frame to draw the eye to the village below.

↻ This photograph of moorland in Cumbria was taken with the telephoto end of a zoom to pick out details in the scenery. Notice how the meandering dry-stone wall has been included in the foreground to draw the eye into the scene.

➲ Blue skies can make stunning backdrops, so make sure you make the most of them by using a punchy colour film. If you have a compact that accepts filters, fit a polarizing filter to further saturate the colours.

↻ Including the reflection of the mountains in the water has added an extra dimension to this shot of Lake Mackenzie on South Island in New Zealand.

interesting cloud formations, place the horizon along the lower third. Look for interesting features in the landscape – a meandering river, a stone wall, boulders or a path – that will help to lead the eye into the frame. If one feature acts as a focal point in the composition, such as a lone building or a solitary tree, try to position it off centre.

Include objects that add scale to the scene. It's pointless filling the frame with sweeping hills if it's impossible to tell how large they are. Incorporating people, trees or cars in the composition helps to give an idea of scale, as does an isolated farmhouse or small village.

THE VIEWPOINT

When you come across a scene with photographic promise, try to resist the temptation to start snapping straightaway. By spending a few minutes simply perusing the view from different vantage points and levels you are more likely to find the best spot from which to take the photograph.

This position is known as the viewpoint and plays an important role in good landscape photography. Often, moving only a few steps in a particular direction or getting slightly closer to the scene can be enough to improve the balance and composition of the image. Minor shifts in

position may also be all that is necessary to exclude distracting objects, such as overhanging branches, from the frame.

Good landscape shots can also be the result of adopting an unusual angle, such as crouching low on the ground or shooting from a high position. Low viewpoints make foreground subjects appear larger than their surroundings and are effective if a dramatic sky is included in the frame. Shooting from a high viewpoint, with the camera pointing downward, works to shorten the gaps between objects positioned one in front of the other, a visual effect that is especially apparent if you are using a zoom at a telephoto setting.

↷ Brighton is one of Britain's most popular beach resorts, with miles of coastline and a famous pier. A wide-angle lens was used to take this shot of Brighton at the height of summer and shows a beach full of sunbathers in the foreground. The line of the beach has been deliberately angled to lead the eye towards the pier at the top of the frame.

↺ Although the cathedral in this scene constitutes only a small part of the photograph, the eye is unconsciously led to it by the dark trench in the foreground and also because it is the only feature in the frame that sticks out into the sky.

↻ Telephoto lenses can be used to take captivating landscapes such as this scene in southern Spain, where the effect of the lens has made the distant hills seem to stack up one on top of the other. The foreground includes a number of houses to add some scale to the backdrop.

Top tip
■ If you're planning to cover a large area on foot consider investing in a monopod which also doubles up as a walking stick.

Camera
Any type of camera is suitable but one with a wide-angle lens will give you the most panoramic shot and will allow you to include plenty of foreground detail to give a good sense of scale and distance. However, a telephoto zoom can be extremely useful if you want to isolate individual elements and will compress perspective to make parts of the scene, such as a range of mountains, appear crowded together. A tripod helps to eliminate camera shake and is invaluable when light levels are low.

Film

Any type of film can be used, but start with colour print or slide film to record the colours in the scene. Choose a slow- or medium-speed film for accurate colour reproduction. The panoramic format is perfect for landscapes, so if you own an APS camera use this format as often as possible. Black-and-white film can result in dramatic and atmospheric shots, helping to emphasize the natural tones and textures of elements such as rocks, water and grass.

Exposure

Bright sky can fool the camera's metering system into underexposing the scene, so you need to be careful if you're including a lot of sky in the frame. The easiest way around this is to point the camera slightly towards the ground until the sky isn't in the frame, then, with the camera aiming at a distant subject, press the shutter button to the halfway position. This will take an exposure reading without the sky in the frame and focus the lens to infinity. With the button still pressed, recompose the scene to your liking and take the shot.

PROJECTS

COUNTRYSIDE Capture three different images of the countryside. This could mean photographing the same area in different weather conditions or at different times of the year. Aim for each picture to reveal new facets of the countryside's beauty.

COASTLINES Visit your local seaside resort or beach and take a wide-angle picture to show a large expanse of the coastline. Try to include something of interest on the horizon, such as a pier or a rocky cliff face.

TELEPHOTO LANDSCAPE Take two pictures with your zoom compact at the telephoto end of the range. Look for distant objects such as hills or mountains to add scale to the shot. For one of the shots try to create the effect known as perspective compression, in which subjects at varying distances appear to be stacked close to each other. ■

↻ You don't have to include huge, sweeping vistas to produce dramatic shots. A telephoto lens was used to pick out this solitary tree, helping to draw attention to the remote, rugged landscape beyond.

↻ The panoramic format is ideal when you want to include large expanses of sky and water, as in this photograph of Sydney harbour, Australia.

↺ A wide-angle lens was the ideal choice for this sweeping seascape of Gibralter. Notice how the Rock has been positioned to the left of the frame.

↻ The success of this well-composed shot of Ayers Rock in Australia owes much to the contrasting colours of the sky, rock and foreground.

Q&A: Landscapes

Should I keep the horizon in the centre of the frame?

You can do, although it's not always the best option. For well-composed landscapes apply the rule of thirds: place the horizon in the bottom third of the frame if there are subjects such as trees above the horizon, and in the top third if you have plenty of foreground detail.

Any other tips for composition?

Look for walls, rivers or other man-made or natural elements which will help to lead the eye into the photograph. These are usually positioned in the foreground of the frame and are an excellent aid for leading the viewer into the image.

Is it worth taking landscapes in bad weather?

Definitely. A stormy sky, with its foreboding grey and black clouds, can add real atmosphere to a landscape. For a really moody result use very fast colour or black-and-white film.

Can I take landscapes with the camera in its upright position?

Yes, there are times when taking pictures with the camera in the upright position produces a more pleasing composition, so don't be afraid to try it out.

People

No two humans are the same, so it is little wonder that people are the most enduringly popular subjects for photography. By developing your portrait technique you will begin to take pictures that offer a unique insight into the character of the person on the other side of the lens.

Displaying an enormous range of emotions, expressions and individual traits, people provide an endless source of fascination and inspiration for the observer. With so many different cultures and personalities to explore, you should have no trouble finding inspiration for some exciting and unique people shots.

Of the many ways of taking pictures of people, portraiture is perhaps the most popular. The two main types of portrait are the formal set-up, which is a one-on-one between the photographer and the subject, and the environmental portrait, in which the subject's surroundings are included in the frame.

Candid photography involves taking pictures of people when they are unaware that you are doing so. The subjects, oblivious of the camera, are at ease, so the shots often have a refreshing spontaneity and immediacy.

And let's not forget children – one of the most photogenic of all subjects and the reason why so many people buy compact cameras in the first place. Taking successful pictures of kids can be as fun as it is challenging.

PROJECTS
Unless you're a hermit you should come into contact with people every day, so finding some suitable subjects shouldn't be too difficult.

PORTRAITS Find a male and female subject and take three pictures of each in different poses. The subjects should appear relaxed and comfortable. Next, photograph someone close to you and try to produce a portrait that looks completely different to any picture of them that you have taken before.

ENVIRONMENTAL PORTRAITS Take four environmental portraits. Two should be of people you know, the other two of people you have never spoken to before until you ask their permission to take the shot.

CANDIDS Spend a few hours in a busy area and take four candids. Good subjects could include a street entertainer, a policeman or a person waiting for someone else. Remember to be as inconspicuous as possible.

CHILDREN Take a set of three pictures of two different children. One shot should feature a child posing, another should show the subject at play and for the third you should try to capture the child with an amusing expression on their face.

➲ Establishing strong eye contact is an important part of a good portrait. Waiting until supermodel Claudia Schiffer looked in the direction of the camera before snapping this shot was vital, especially as one eye was obscured by hair.

PORTRAITURE

You shouldn't take a portrait simply to record how your subject looks. For a portrait to be successful, the photograph should reveal something of the person's character and personality. This isn't as easy as it might sound, and for a portrait to work really well, a trust must be established between the photographer and the subject. Without this trust, the person being photographed will not feel relaxed and the portrait will look forced and unnatural. With close friends and family this is usually less of a problem, but with people you don't know or those who are particularly camera-shy, you will need to work that much harder to develop this trust and put them at ease.

Taking a decent portrait, then, is as much about how you interact with your subject and control the situation as it is about good photographic technique. There are a number of things you can do to make your subject feel more comfortable and help to make the session run smoothly. Have the camera set up on a tripod where you plan to take the pictures and make sure that everything is ready before the session begins.

Don't start taking pictures straightaway. Instead, make the subject feel at home by talking to them for a few minutes. Keep chatting as the photo session is about to start, as this is the point where people usually feel most nervous. While your subject is talking, look through the

↻ There's no need to fill the frame with your subject. Keep your eye out for potential backdrops. This abstract shot was taken by tilting the camera at an angle to make it appear as if the building is pointing up to the sky and placing the subject in the middle of the frame.

↻ Camera shake is usually something to be avoided but it can occasionally be used creatively. By waiting until the frame was filled with people and taking the picture while moving backward, the photographer has added motion to this crowd scene.

↺ A good portrait should reveal something of the personality of the subject. This gentleman has been collecting exotic fish for many years, so it made sense to include evidence of his hobby in the photo.

viewfinder and compose the shot. When you start taking the photographs, you can take your eye away from the viewfinder and look at the subject. Establishing direct eye-to-eye contact in this way means you can keep talking to the subject while taking pictures.

Take a five-minute break every twenty minutes and end the session after an hour, by which time you should have covered most poses.

Camera

A compact with a telephoto zoom is the best choice as it allows you to keep some distance between you and the subject, making them feel less intimidated. Also, the perspective of a telephoto lens is more flattering for portraits. Use the portrait mode on your camera if it has one.

Film

Portraits work equally well in colour or black and white; experiment with both and see which you prefer. ISO 100 film is perfectly acceptable, but also think about using one of the fast and grainy ISO 1600/3200 films for extra mood.

Exposure

If you're shooting indoors, position your subject by a window so that the light shining through will provide a flattering effect. Outdoors, make sure that they are not looking directly into the light, as this will cause them to squint. Position them in the shade and use fill-in flash to remove any shadows on their face and to add an attractive catchlight to their eyes. Invest in a small, portable reflector to reflect light back onto the face.

ENVIRONMENTAL PORTRAITS

Sometimes the place where a person lives or works can reveal a lot about their personality. Not only that, but it sheds a little light onto how a person lives, something that isn't usually possible with a straightforward portrait. This is what environmental portraiture is all about, photographing your subject in their surroundings and so revealing a small part of their lives – a gardener leaning on a spade, for instance, a fisherman standing next to his boat or a sportsman surrounded by trophies.

One advantage of this type of photography is that the subject will feel more relaxed in familiar surroundings, making it easier to get a more natural portrait. Bear in mind that an

environmental portrait does not have to be serious. Adding some humour and having your subject do something unexpected can work well. An action picture can be more interesting than a static one. A teacher writing lines on the blackboard would make a more interesting image, say, than having him or her simply sitting at a desk.

Camera
Any type of camera is suitable. A wide-angle lens allows you to include plenty of the subject's surroundings in the frame.

Film
Both colour and black and white are suitable for environmental portraits. Often you will be taking pictures indoors so a fast film is more suitable. Black-and-white film brings a documentary feel to the shot, but use colour if the surroundings are particularly vibrant.

Exposure
Fill-in flash is useful for outdoor shots as it brings out details in the subject's surroundings as well as in their face. Indoors, using slow-sync flash can produce a good balance between flash and ambient light.

↻ Sometimes it's worth making the working environment, rather than the subject, the central feature of the shot. Taken inside the cockpit of a plane, the photographer has focused on the instrument panel rather than the pilots. The dials and displays have thus become the main focus of attention, with the pilots at the side framing the shot and appearing slightly out of focus.

↻ ↺ These two shots were taken only feet apart but look completely different. Shooting from a distance has allowed five members of the pit crew relaxing before the start of the race to be included in the frame. Moving closer and using the zoom has picked out another member of the team having a conversation via his radio.

↺ Photograph this man on his own and it's impossible to work out what he does for a living; include his surroundings in the frame and it becomes obvious. This is what environmental portraiture is all about. The composition of the picture has been carefully thought out, with the market-stall owner on the far left of the picture while his stall takes up the rest of the frame.

CANDID SHOTS

This is probably the easiest type of people photograph to take because there's no need to set up the shot. All you need to do is carry your camera around with you and keep your eyes open for potential subjects. A good candid shot is about capturing the moment, so when a good photo opportunity arises you will need to act fast.

Because candid photography is so spontaneous, the results are often more revealing than with other types of

⟳ People waiting or sitting often make good candid subjects, as witnessed in this picture of a lady enjoying a moment of quiet contemplation.

portraiture. When people are unaware that they are having their picture taken, you are more likely to capture them behaving completely naturally. Candid shots of weddings, for instance, can often provide a livelier and more natural record of the day than any number of staged photographs.

You should practise your candid photography in places where there are plenty of people about, such as a busy street or a social event. However, there is more to candid photography than simply firing off several frames with the camera pointing aimlessly into a crowd of people. Timing is essential to capture the moment when the subject is in the right position.

One good approach is to find a vantage point that will give you a good view of the area around you – perhaps a café with outdoor tables facing the street. You can then peruse the scene with less chance of being detected.

⟳ This lady and her children were caught unawares feeding pigeons. Using a zoom isolated the group and the hundreds of birds surrounding them. A fast ISO 400 film meant a fast shutter speed could be used, resulting in many of the birds being frozen in mid-air.

◖ A good candid picture should raise questions, so look for subjects that will excite the curiosity of the viewer and make them want to learn more about the life of the person in the shot.

Alternatively, wander around a particular area to see if you can spot any potential subjects. A good place to try this is at an outdoor market. Walk about and examine the characters working and shopping at the stalls. You're bound to find several suitable candid opportunities.

Often potential pictures present themselves in a split second, so you should always be aware of the surroundings and have the camera ready before the moment has passed. It's worth remembering that some people might object to having their picture taken – especially by a complete stranger – so avoid photographing anyone who looks less than friendly and if you are confronted explain what you are doing.

Camera
A compact with a good zoom range is handy as it allows you to pull in distant subjects. More importantly, it allows you to stay a fair distance from the subject, reducing the risk of being spotted.

Film
Both colour or black and white are suitable, although black-and-white films add a documentary feel to candids. Use a fast film to prevent the flash from firing. ISO 400 should be fine, but in less than bright conditions use an ISO 800 film.

Exposure
Make sure that the flash is switched off. The subject is usually too far away for the flash to be effective and the flash could alert the subject to your presence.

Top tips
- Practise your candid technique on unsuspecting friends or family and see how often you can take pictures without getting caught.

- Stay inconspicuous by remaining in the same spot for a few minutes.

CHILDREN

Many people buy a camera especially to photograph their children growing up, and a compact is ideal for capturing those spontaneous moments.

Most children are used to having their picture taken, so aren't as camera-shy as adults. Children seem to have a limitless number of expressions that change like the wind, so watch them play and be patient because a great picture is usually never far away. One minute they may look happy, the next pensive, the next tearful. So keep your camera handy and be ready to fire away.

Remember that children have a short attention span, so trying to get them to pose for more than a few minutes is doomed to failure as they are bound to get restless and bored. Leaving them to their own devices is your best option.

Rather than towering over your subject and forcing them to look up, you should try to get down to a child's eye-level by shooting from a kneeling position.

Top tips

■ Props, such as balloons or toys, can detract the child's attention from the camera and help to create a colourful composition.

■ Children don't like sitting still for long, so don't ask a child to pose until you're ready. You'll probably find that the best shots are those that are not set up.

Even if you don't have children of your own, there's no reason why you can't record some exciting photographic moments. When travelling abroad, for instance, taking photos of local children in their own environment can give a good insight into the culture of the country and result in some fascinating shots. A carnival or fun fair can also provide the perfect backdrop for some colourful and spontaneous shots of children.

➲ It's not always easy to keep children still long enough to take a decent picture, so it's worth waiting for moments when they are eating or taking a rest.

↻ Always have a camera at the ready and be prepared to snap away whenever an opportunity arises. By crouching down to the subject's level you will make the child feel more at ease and get a more natural shot.

Camera

Any type of compact is ideal. A camera with a wide-angle lens is useful for taking indoor pictures in cramped conditions. However, if the subject is camera-shy a zoom lens allows you to keep a good distance between you and the child.

Film

Colour or black and white is suitable.

Exposure

Children are prone to red eye, so make sure you have the red-eye reduction facility activated to minimize the problem. If the child is playing, use a fast film to increase the shutter speed. ■

Q&A: People

What's the single most important thing in a portrait?

Strong eye contact from the subject is generally agreed to be the number one rule. However, rules can be broken and it is possible to capture really arresting portraits without there being any eye contact. Having the eyes looking left or right works well if the expression on the face is appropriate, for instance if the subject looks as if they're trying to spy on the person next to them.

What else should I remember?

Always try to ensure the subject is relaxed, or else the picture will appear unnatural.

Where should I focus?

Because the eyes are the most important feature, lock the focus on them and recompose the picture to your liking.

Any tips to ensure I show the subject in the best possible light?

A subject's nose can often look too prominent on film. To counteract this, use a telephoto setting on your zoom compact if you have one. Position the face so that it is looking straight at the camera – if the face is angled the nose becomes more prominent. To minimize a double chin, ask the subject to lift their head slightly. Switch the flash off to avoid reflections in spectacles, or ask the subject to remove them.

Still life

Mastering a good still-life technique takes time and practice. This is not about point-and-shoot photography, but if you persevere, the results can be extremely rewarding. Even the most mundane objects can be transformed into truly unique images.

Still life is quite an involved type of photography because in addition to taking the picture, you also need to set up the subject, make sure you have a pleasing composition and pay close attention to the lighting. This means that it can be quite a time-consuming process, but the beauty of this technique is that you will have complete control over every stage of the process. So if it's raining outside, turn off the TV and practise your still-life photography instead.

Taking great still lifes requires fine-tuning your skills at preparation and untapping your creativity. You should take things one step at a time and build up your experience. Pay close attention to detail in the scene, keep things simple and don't overelaborate.

Making the best use of lighting can be tricky enough even with an expensive camera outfit and studio lights, so getting a decent result with a compact or digital camera requires practice and patience.

Start by taking a picture of a relatively easy subject, a vase of flowers, say, or a bottle of wine. Position the still life by a window for attractive sidelighting and in front of a plain background to keep the composition uncluttered. Place a reflector, such as a mirror or a white sheet, outside the frame to fill in some of the shadows. Alternatively, you could use the window as a backdrop and place the subject directly in front of it. If the subject is solid the result will be a silhouette, but if it's a transparent object such as a bottle the backlighting can produce wonderful patterns in the glass or plastic.

○ This arrangement of shells, pine cones and potpourri took only minutes to get ready, but the result is a pleasing combination of textures, shapes and vibrant colours.

Achieving a good composition is an important aspect of a successful still life. Because most still lifes consist of several objects, you must make sure that the picture looks well balanced. It's worth mounting the camera on a tripod so you can return to the still life from time to time to make any necessary adjustments.

Look for subjects that will tell a story, such as a pair of football boots with a trophy next to them to record a sporting success. A still life with an old photograph of a man or woman and some letters will conjure up an image of a past love affair.

C A row of glass bottles filled with coloured liquids and shot in natural daylight has produced a simple but eye-catching still life.

Spend a few moments in each room of your house searching for potential subjects. If you have a bookcase in your dining room or study, why not fill the frame with a collection of books; in the kitchen you could arrange some vegetables and a knife on a chopping board. Raid the attic for any old memorabilia that could be used for a nostalgic black-and-white shot. Venture out into the garden for further inspiration. As well as photographing flowers, berries or leaves, you could consider basing a still life around some muddy boots or rusty tools.

Camera

Any camera is suitable so long as you are able to switch off the flash. A tripod is essential as it allows you to leave the camera in a fixed position and accurately compose the still life. It also means that shooting at slow shutter speeds will not result in camera shake. A close-up facility is useful if the objects included in your still life are small.

Film

Choose colour or black-and-white film if working in daylight. If using tungsten lighting, black-and-white film should be used. A medium film speed such as ISO 100 is recommended. If you are using diffuse daylight you should also think about trying out an ultra fast ISO 1600 film as the coarse grain and softer colours will bring a romantic quality to the image.

Still life photography gives you the perfect opportunity to try out different films. It's worth taking identical pictures

↻ Imaginative still-life subjects can appear in the most unexpected places, so it's worth keeping your camera with you at all times. This shot was taken in a supermarket in Florida the day before Halloween, using an APS compact in the Panoramic print format.

Top Tip

■ Switch the flash off when you are photographing reflective objects such as metal or glass, otherwise the reflection will ruin the shot.

with a selection of films to find out which produce the most interesting results.

Exposure

Because you don't have enough control over the integral flash to know what its effect on the scene will be, your best option is to rely on daylight shining through a window and lighting the subject from the side. This actually works quite well because the diffuse lighting can add to the overall atmosphere of the shot. However, it does mean that you are limited to using particular windows at certain times of the day when the sun is in the appropriate position.

You have more scope with the lighting if you are using black-and-white film. You can use tungsten lighting as the warmer colour this type of light produces will not show up on the film. So, if you feel really confident, use a couple of table lamps as the lighting source. Another option is to buy light bulbs that produce daylight balanced light. These can be used in ordinary household lamps and will allow you to take pictures indoors without a colour cast appearing.

PROJECTS

Take five still lifes in your home, each showing a different subject. Include such things as flowers, fruit or vegetables and some bottles or jars. Use a variety of film, including colour, black and white and some high-speed grainy film. ■

↻ Make the most of festivals such as Christmas to create a seasonal still life. Careful composition was vital to the success of this image, with the baubles positioned to produce a balanced image. The flash and room lights were all switched off so that the tree's lights could reveal a warm, orange glow.

Ↄ Lighting plays a major part in a successful still life. The orange cast of this shot demonstrates the effect of taking pictures in artificial lighting without flash. However, in this instance the orange cast adds atmosphere to the still life, rather than spoiling it. Using flash would remove the cast but would also fill in the shadows of the eye and nasal sockets, making the subject look less intimidating.

Q&A: Still life

What subjects make good still lifes?

Colour is an important element of many still lifes, which is why flowers are popular subjects. Patterns also play their part, so keep an eye out for a collection of items, such as a set of coloured pencils, which could make a photogenic subject.

Are still lifes always set up?

It's fair to say that most still lifes are set up by the photographer rather than discovered by chance. However, that's not to say you won't unexpectedly come across something in your home, or even outdoors, that would make an exciting still life.

Does my camera need a close-up facility?

If your subjects are small then a close-up facility will be necessary. However, if you're shooting something like a vase of flowers, then this feature isn't required.

I would like to produce some abstract still lifes – any ideas for subject matter?

The only limit is your own imagination. You could try photographing a golf umbrella from the inside. Open it up in bright daylight, so that the sun shines through the material, and capture the colourful stripes.

Close-ups

Whether it's to photograph butterflies in the garden or to capture the minute detail of a flower, a close-up facility is a very useful feature to have on your camera. Although taking high quality close-ups requires practice, the results can be rewarding and revealing.

There are countless subjects that can be used for this type of photography. The natural world offers a wealth of close-up opportunities, with bark, insects and feathers being just a few of the many possibilities. Even things that look relatively uninspiring to the naked eye, such as pebbles, rocks or leaves, can reveal wonderful intricacies of pattern and colour when taken from a close-up range. Indoors, close-ups of children's toys or decorative patterns can yield interesting results, or you might want to record the subject of a hobby with close-ups of postage stamps or old coins.

One of the main challenges facing the close-up photographer is the lack of depth-of-field. The closer you are to a

↻ The very shallow depth of field of close-up work means that accurate focusing is critical to producing sharp results.

Framing the subject

It's easy to frame the subject using a digital camera with an LCD monitor or a digital single-lens reflex, because the image you see is what is captured by the CCD. With 35mm and APS compacts, as well as digital cameras lacking an LCD monitor, accurate framing of the subject isn't quite as straightforward. This is because the viewfinder you look through shows a slightly different view of the subject than the lens. This difference is only apparent with close-up subjects and is known as parallax error. Many cameras have extra lines at the top and side of the viewfinder which are known as parallax markings. These are used as a guide for positioning the subject in the centre of the frame when shooting close-ups. The subject is placed in the centre of the frame as normal and the shutter button pressed halfway down to lock on the subject. Using the guide lines, a slight adjustment is then made to compensate for parallax error. Although it appears in the viewfinder that the subject is no longer in the centre of the frame, it will be correctly positioned in the actual photograph.

subject, the shallower the depth-of-field becomes. With close-ups this can mean that the depth-of-field measures only a few millimetres, so you will need to be very careful with the focusing otherwise the picture will appear blurred.

Camera

Many compacts offer a close-up mode, usually depicted with a flower icon on the camera, which allows photography as close as 30 or 40cm from the subject.

However, digital cameras have the advantage, with most models getting as close as 10 or 20cm from the subject.

If your camera allows you to select the aperture, use the minimum aperture to provide as much depth-of-field as possible.

Film

Colour film is the best choice if you're planning to photograph flowers or insects. Use a medium- to fast-speed film (ISO 200 or ISO 400) as this will increase the shutter speed and reduce the risk of camera shake.

Exposure

Getting the lighting right can be a problem with close-up photography. Although you can try using the built-in flash, you will probably find that it overexposes the picture. Instead, it is best to switch the flash off and rely on ambient light instead. When you are photographing close-ups indoors, shoot next to a north-facing window to provide an even and diffuse light source. This will usually result in a slow shutter speed, so you should use a tripod to avoid camera shake. Another useful accessory to consider is a reflector which can be used to fill-in shadows and provide a more even illumination. When taking a close-up, make sure that you do not throw a shadow over the subject.

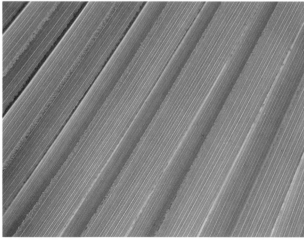

↷ When you are taking close-ups of flowers, always keep an eye out for sunlight passing through the petals. The light at the back has added a luminosity to the colours of this flower.

↻ Focusing on a small section of this leaf draws attention to the vibrant colour and intricate pattern of the subject.

PROJECTS
OVERCOMING PARALLAX PROBLEMS
This first project is aimed at getting you used to composing the picture so that the subject appears in the centre of the photograph. Take a small object such as a flower or a shell and place it on a plain surface. Take a series of pictures, each time positioning it in a different part of the viewfinder – in the centre, toward each corner, then along the edges, for example. Write down the subject's position for each frame, then have the film processed. When the photos are returned, you will be able to compare the notes with the position of the subject in the photo to work out where to place the subject in future close-ups.

FLOWERS AND FUNGI Take a series of pictures featuring flowers and fungi. Look for interesting combinations of colour, pattern and texture, and try shooting from different angles.

Top tip
- Check the camera's instructions to find out what magnification the lens is capable of. It is usually displayed as a fraction. For instance, 0.25x means the subject will appear $\frac{1}{4}$ life-size on the film; 0.125x means the subject will appear $\frac{1}{8}$ life-size on the film.

INSECTS Scour your garden or local park and photograph four different types of insect. One should be a colourful subject such as a butterfly.

STILL LIFE Set up your own still life and produce some interesting close-ups taken from different angles. Suitable props could include coloured pencils, paper clips, stamps, beads, coloured glass or coins, or you could try an arrangement of small fruit such as berries. ■

↻ To capture a subject this small requires a camera with a close-up mode that allows you to get within around 30cm of the subject. Shooting against an uncluttered background and using a shallow depth-of-field has emphasized the purple flower with the bee sitting upon it.

Black-and-white documentary

There are times when including colour in your photographs can distract attention from the main impact of an image. Using black-and-white film often adds a graphic resonance and atmosphere to your pictures, especially when you want to record an event or tell a story.

Black-and-white film is widely used by professionals but it is often overlooked by amateur photographers, especially those using compact cameras. However, there are plenty of good films on the market and it is well worth giving this medium a go. Black-and-white film has a unique quality of its own, especially for taking documentary photographs, a technique often referred to as 'reportage' photography. The ease and speed of use of a compact camera makes it an ideal choice for taking black-and-white images.

ↄ The rule of thirds has been used to good effect in this picture of two French policemen returning to their vehicle. Both men are on the lower left third of the frame, while the van is in the upper right third.

↷ Busy street scenes, such as this shot taken in Pakistan, make good subjects for black-and-white photography because the eye is not distracted by a myriad of colours.

➲ Black-and-white film can bring a timeless feel to your pictures. This monochrome portrait of an elderly Turkish couple could have been taken any time in the last fifty years.

You will also find that tricky lighting conditions are much less of a problem than with colour, as black-and-white film has a wide exposure latitude and exposure alterations can be made at the printing stage.

One of the main reasons why black-and-white film works so well for documentary or news pictures is that there are no colours to detract from the scene's impact, forcing the viewer to focus on the subject. Also, black-and-white pictures have a timeless feel to them, which adds interest and atmosphere to the results.

Taking great pictures with black-and-white film requires plenty of practice and a good eye for detail. The secret is to try and imagine the scene in black and white, concentrating on such things as tone, shape and texture.

Documentary photography is about having the ability to spot photogenic moments. When photographing everyday scenes, look for interesting locations that show locals at work or play. If you're in a foreign country, black-and-white images are a good way to encapsulate the spirit of another culture.

If you are covering newsworthy events, such as a political march, you will need to be ready to shoot the moment an

opportunity arises. You should also think about how you can cover the event from an unusual angle to add extra impact to the shot. Get in close to the subjects to fill the frame with faces and movement, or move a distance away to convey the scale of the event and provide visual evidence of the location.

Camera

Any type of compact is suitable. A wide-angle lens is ideal for including plenty of the scene in the frame, but a zoom

⊙ Trips abroad provide plenty of scope to perfect your black-and-white photography and record the lives of the local people, as with these street singers snapped in a Paris street.

⊃ Pictures of pale or grey subjects taken in overcast conditions may look drab and lifeless in colour, but black-and-white film has given definition to this image of Hungarian bathers playing chess.

If you are photographing an outside event, try to capture different views of the scene, as the photographer has done in this series of shots of a protest march in central London.

↻ A wide-angle lens was used to include the entire length of Nelson's Column in the frame, providing a backdrop to the line of policemen in the foreground as well as a record of the scene's location.

↪ Getting much closer to the line of policemen has produced a very different picture. There is now little evidence of where the picture was taken, but this has been compensated for by the range of expressions on the policemen's faces.

↻ The same location, taken a few minutes later. Getting in close with a wide-angle lens has recorded the faces of the marchers, as well as the banners indicating what they are protesting against.

enables you to pick out individual elements. Some digital cameras can be set to take pictures in black and white, although it is easy to manipulate a colour picture on the computer.

Film

There are several films to choose from. Start with an ISO 400, which offers a good combination of speed and quality.

Exposure

Black-and-white print film has a wide exposure latitude, so being critical with the exposure isn't always necessary. However, you should try to meter from a mid-tone whenever possible. Black-and-white film has an advantage over colour when taking pictures indoors because the problems associated with colour casts from artificial lighting do not apply.

PROJECTS

EVERYDAY LIFE Take two shots that show scenes of everyday life in your local town. One shot should include a landmark or other reference to indicate the scene's location, the other should be an ordinary scene that could be taken in any town or city.

A MAJOR EVENT Take two pictures that provide a record of a major event. If you are taking pictures of a crowd, for instance, aim to include a large area of the scene and then zoom in close to focus on one or two individual faces. ■

Q&A: Black-and-white documentary

If my camera is loaded with colour film when I take some pictures, can I get them processed as black-and-white prints?

Yes. Some labs will produce black-and-white prints from colour negative or slide films but it is relatively expensive and the results aren't as good as for pictures taken on black-and-white film. If you own a computer and scanner, you can easily manipulate your colour photos.

Is black-and-white processing readily available and how do costs compare with those for colour film?

Many high street and mail-order labs can handle black-and-white film, but processing usually costs a little more and takes a little longer than with colour print.

Are there any restrictions on taking photographs of the police or armed forces?

In some countries you could encounter problems if you photograph any police or military personnel, so it is always wise to ask for permission before you start.

Travel

Holidays often provide the ideal opportunity to take plenty of snaps, but all too often the results can be disappointing and uninspiring. This section will show you how you can record memories of places that you will want to return to again and again.

Every country has its own unique culture, so travel photography offers enormous scope for creative picture-taking. There's a wealth of subjects to cover – from the local people and their customs to the architecture and landscape – so make sure you pack your camera next time you go travelling.

The techniques for covering these subjects are dealt with elsewhere in the book but here are a few hints and tips for photographers about to travel.

Make sure you obtain a good guide book and a map before you travel. These are invaluable for locating places of interest and will save you time travelling

from one place to another. Take plenty of 'postcard-type' scenes that make the location of the photograph instantly recognizable. It's pointless visiting a country thousands of miles away if nobody can tell from the pictures where you have been. Look for obvious landmarks – if you're in New York take pictures of the Statue of Liberty; if you're in Sydney, Australia, make sure you capture the famous Sydney Opera House. Look at postcards of a particular building or landmark and think about how you can come up with something different by shooting from an unusual angle or at another time of day.

Once you have taken pictures of the obvious landmarks, you can then branch out and look for the more subtle images that will encapsulate the atmosphere of the place. Taking pictures of the local people as they go about their everyday life is a popular approach and you will often find street markets, festivals and other busy places offer many good opportunities for this type of picture.

Architecture varies from culture to culture, so always photograph some of the local buildings. Religious buildings, in particular, offer many visual delights, so make these among your first ports of call. You should also include plenty of shots of the landscape and native wildlife.

☾ Careful composition has allowed the silhouette of the camel and people to be included in the frame, providing a vital clue to the scale of the pyramid.

➲ Don't be afraid to use the panoramic format in an upright position. In this shot, the pedestal and background have been included to add some scale to the subject.

Camera

A wide-angle lens will allow you to take landscape pictures and fit entire buildings in the frame. A zoom lens permits you to pick out details in the scene and take candid pictures of the locals.

Film

Because there are so many different subjects to cover when travelling, aim to take a variety of film with you. As well as colour and black-and-white film, you should also try colour infrared film (see pages 178–179).

Exposure

Take care with exposure when you are photographing in bright, sunny conditions or snow-filled scenes, otherwise you risk underexposing the shot. Avoid the problem by taking a spot-meter reading from a mid-tone. Or exclude bright areas such as sky from the frame when locking the exposure/focus by partially depressing the shutter button. You also need to be careful when shooting metallic objects such as statues, because their bright reflections can cause the camera to underexpose.

PROJECT

On your next holiday, take four pictures of the area you are visiting. At least one should be a shot of a building, another a famous landmark and one should include a local person at work or play. ∎

↺ Look for landscapes that are dramatically different from anything you are used to back home. This shot of Machu Picchu, in Peru, was taken from a high vantage point to capture the stunning panorama.

⤴ This picture of bathing elephants taken in Sri Lanka offers an invaluable glimpse into the way of life in another country.

↻ Photographs of public transport can also provide a unique record of a foreign culture. These Tuk Tuks are a popular, if dangerous, form of taxi in Thailand and were shot from the back of another Tuk Tuk.

C You don't always have to be different. The Taj Mahal in India has been shot from this position thousands of times before, but there's no denying the result is spectacular. Note how the main subject has been positioned in the centre of the frame, emphasizing the symmetry of the architecture.

Animals

Pictures of family pets make enduringly popular subjects for the photo album, but you should also aim to include other members of the animal kingdom. Zoos, bird sanctuaries, parks, even your back garden can be excellent hunting grounds for some great animal shots.

With the possible exception of children, no other subject demands as much patience from a photographer as animals. Most animals won't pose to order, so you will need to be alert and ready to shoot as soon as the opportunity presents itself.

PETS

For most of us a pet is another member of the family and while there is nothing wrong with a quick snapshot, taking a little more time and care can yield a pet picture that will be looked at and loved for many years to come.

It's very difficult to get your pet to sit and pose – even a highly trained dog won't sit to attention forever. There are some tricks you can try, however, to get your animal's attention. Frame the subject in the viewfinder then squeak a favourite toy just above your head. This usually makes the animal look up and you'll be able to snap off a quick shot.

Remember always to treat your pet with respect. Never force it to do anything it doesn't want to and do not get angry with it if it seems reluctant or scared to take part.

Camera

Any type of camera is suitable, but a zoom compact is invaluable as it allows you to include the entire animal if used at the wide-angle end, or you can zoom in and fill the frame with the pet's face without having to get too close to the animal and scaring it away.

Film

Most animal pictures look best in colour, especially if you have a brightly coloured pet such as a parrot or goldfish. However, don't be put off from trying out black-and-white film. Any speed of film between ISO 100 and ISO 800 is suitable.

Exposure

So long as your subject is within a couple

⊙ Getting a cat's attention for long enough can be difficult but a squeaky toy behind the camera worked on this occasion. Using flash has darkened the background and made the cat stand out more.

↻ It's unusual to be looking up at a dog, but trying out this technique can produce great results. Here the subject was framed with the sun behind it to highlight the fur on its head. Fill-in flash was used to provide detail on the face.

of metres of you, it's always worth using the flash, whether you're shooting indoors or out. Outdoors, the flash will provide fill-in on the animal's face and also add a catchlight to the eyes. Indoors, the flash will prevent the photographs from appearing orange due to the artificial lights. You should use the red-eye reduction mode on the flash to contract the animal's pupils. ■

ZOO ANIMALS

A visit to a zoo or safari park offers a good opportunity to observe the fascinating behaviour of many exotic species at close range and capture animals on film without travelling thousands of miles. One of the main challenges posed by this type of photography is that views of the animals are often obstructed by fencing, so you will need to get plenty of practice to perfect your technique. Find out when the animals' feeding times are, as these can provide some of the best moments for natural, spontaneous pictures.

Camera

A camera with a powerful telephoto zoom is ideal as it will allow you to zoom in and tightly frame the animals.

Film

The diversity of colours on show demands colour film. Because you will often be using the telephoto end of your zoom, a fast film such as ISO 400 or ISO 800 is recommended.

Exposure

Because the subjects will often be outside the flash range, switch the autoflash off. Also, if you're shooting through bars or fencing, the flash light would reflect off the metal and ruin the image.

Shooting through fencing presents two problems. The first is that the fencing obscures the image; the second is that it can interfere with the autofocus system. Using the lens at a telephoto setting can often overcome these problems. By zooming in on the subject, the fencing is often sufficiently blurred as to be almost invisible on the photo. For this to work best, you should stand within a few feet of the fence and there should be as much distance as possible between the animal and the fence.

This technique also helps the autofocus avoid the fence and focus on the animal behind it. If your camera has an infinity lock or manual focus override, you should consider using it. An alternative technique is to focus on something a similar distance away from you as the subject, and while the focus is locked recompose and shoot.

Bear in mind that taking a picture of an animal at rest is obviously easier than trying to track a moving subject. It is also worth visiting the animals shortly after they have fed when they are usually more docile and easier to shoot.

Top tip
- Never take risks by getting too close to the fencing. Always read and follow the zoo's safety procedures.

⌒ Find the right position and it's possible to take zoo pictures that look as if they were shot in the wild. Here a telephoto lens was selected to concentrate on the alligator's head.

⤳ This Barbary ape was caught taking a rest on a telescope in an enclosure on the Rock of Gibraltar.

↺ Although this shot of a sea lion was taken through fencing, the use of a telephoto zoom has eliminated any trace of it.

BIRDS

These are extremely cautious creatures, so photographing them before they fly away can be difficult. Some birds, such as swans or geese, can often be kept close enough by coaxing them with food.

Camera

A camera with a telephoto zoom will let you fill the frame with one bird without having to get too close and scaring it away. But a wide-angle lens is useful if you want to photograph a group of birds together.

Film

Any type of film is suitable, although colour is usually the most appropriate for capturing birdlife. In bright conditions, an ISO 100 film is acceptable but if you intend using the zoom, consider a faster speed, such as ISO 200 or 400.

Exposure

Your camera's metering system should be able to handle most situations. However, if your subject is backlit or predominantly white, take care to avoid underexposure.

PROJECTS

PETS Take a set of four pictures of the family cat or dog (or a friend's pet if you don't have one of your own). Each picture should reveal a different aspect of the animal's personality. For instance, you

could take one picture of the animal at play, another of it resting, a shot of it filling the frame and a final picture taken from an unusual viewpoint.

ZOO ANIMALS Take six pictures, including in your set one big cat, a large mammal, and an ape or monkey. For one or two of the shots, try shooting through glass or the bars of a cage.

BIRDS Photograph three different birds. You can include something as common as a pigeon or a more colourful and exotic species such as a peacock, but make sure you vary the composition and include some close-ups. ■

☾ Swans and geese made photogenic subjects for this ethereal, wintry picture. Most of the birds are concentrated in the central third of the shot and are framed with the lines of trees along the top third of the scene and the edge of the water along the bottom third.

↻ To get this close required a telephoto zoom. Exposure was tricky as the subject was backlit and white, but taking a spot reading from the grey feathers resulted in the correct exposure.

Q&A: Animals

Will the flash harm my pet's eyes?
Flash photography should not cause any discomfort to the animal. Although the flash appears very bright, the actual output is low enough not to damage the eyes.

Are animals prone to red eye?
An animal's eyes can often reflect the flash, although the colour of the reflection is usually yellow or green, rather than red. Use the same procedure to eliminate red-eye reduction as you would with a human subject (see pages 20–21).

What's the best way to photograph a moving animal?
Cameras with servo autofocus are able to adjust the focusing to follow a moving subject. Most compacts aren't able to track a moving subject but there is a way around this. Try focusing on the area of ground in front of the animal and when it is about to reach this point, take the picture.

Is it easy to photograph animals in the wild?
Animals generally shy away from people, so photographing them requires a great deal of patience. Find a place where you know the animal visits and remain in the same position quietly until it reappears.

Architecture

Walk through any town or city and you should be able to find at least one or two buildings with photographic potential. Take a closer look at the street where you live or work and you will probably discover some interesting architectural details that you haven't noticed before.

Architecture is an often overlooked subject for photography but, being static, buildings are relatively easy to shoot and can provide endless scope for great pictures. There are two main approaches to photographing a building. The first is to use a wide-angle lens that captures all, or most, of the building in the frame. The other option is to get in close with a telephoto lens and pick out some of the intricate details and features. Look for repetition in the structure such as pillars or windows which can create some interesting patterns.

A visit to a town or city with a long history can often reveal fascinating architectural treasures. A good starting point is to go to an old church. As well as observing the overall shape and size of the building, look, too, for any interesting details such as gargoyles, windows or intricate patterns in the brickwork.

⟳ A telephoto zoom is ideal for isolating parts of a building. The photographer has shot this railway station from an unusual angle, concentrating on the curves of the roof which contrast with the square panels of the structure.

⊃ Zooming in tight on this bell has resulted in a pleasing composition.

⟲ Shooting from a low viewpoint has exaggerated the shape of these unusual statues and has also caused the pillars behind them to appear to be leaning backward – an effect known as converging verticals.

Modern buildings, with their clean, graphic lines and symmetrical qualities, can also offer a rich source of inspiration for visually arresting photographs.

If you have a zoom compact then it's worth zooming the lens to its maximum telephoto setting to produce pictures showing perspective compression. This is an effect in which buildings appear so close together that they seem to be stacked one against the other. You'll need a powerful zoom to achieve this effect; the more powerful the zoom, the more dramatic the effect.

The time of day and quality of light can have a dramatic impact on a building's appearance. Sidelighting will produce a series of shadows and highlights on brickwork, while direct sun results in bright reflections off windows. A building that looks rather flat and unprepossessing in dull, cloudy weather can be transformed by the late afternoon sunlight, with the brickwork bathed in an attractive golden glow. At night-time, artificial lighting can also radically alter how a building looks, especially if it is lit by coloured floodlights. In the evening, keep an eye out for the golden reflection of the setting sun in windows.

Choosing the right viewpoint is another important consideration. Photographing buildings square on can sometimes make them look rather flat and uninteresting, so you should take time to study the building from different levels and angles

to see how you can capture them in the best possible light. If you want to take a dramatic shot of city skyscrapers, for instance, try lying down on the ground and taking a picture with the lens pointing directly upward and set to wide-angle. This gives the appearance that all the buildings are leaning into the centre of the frame. Alternatively, shoot from a high vantage point with a wide-angle lens to fit in as many of the buildings as possible. If you're shooting a famous landmark that has been photographed countless times before, try to take it from an unusual perspective. Often the best way to do this is to get close and shoot upward with a wide-angle lens, so as to exaggerate the building's shape.

↻ If you photograph rows of buildings with the telephoto end of the zoom you can create an effect known as perspective compression, as witnessed in this shot of a crowded Spanish village where all the buildings seem to be stacked against one another.

Camera
A wide-angle lens will allow you to fit an entire building in the frame while a telephoto zoom will let you home in on details.

Film
Colour or black-and-white film can be used. If you're photographing old buildings try a roll of ultra-fast film for atmospheric, grainy results. Fast film is a good choice if you're using the telephoto end of the zoom.

↻ ↺ Churches and cathedrals offer a rich source of photogenic detail. These two images show how it is possible to take several interesting shots from just one architectural feature. Standing a distance away and using a wide-angle lens has allowed the entire arch to be included in the frame. Moving closer and zooming in on one particular figure has produced an equally pleasing composition.

Exposure

Most architectural subjects are easy to photograph because the grey or brown exterior of the buildings poses no difficulties for the camera's metering system. However, in bright sunlight it's best to lock the focus and meter on part of the subject that doesn't include any windows, then recompose the shot.

PROJECTS

THE INTERIOR AND EXTERIOR OF AN OLD AND A MODERN BUILDING Take two photos of the exterior and interior of an old building. One of the exterior pictures should be a wide-angle shot showing a large amount of the building, the other should be a close-up of some architectural detail. If your subject is a church, for instance, the exterior shots could be of the spire and a close-up of a gargoyle. The interior pictures could include a wide-angle shot of the church's decorated ceiling and a close-up of some detail in the crypt. Once you have completed this set of pictures, repeat the project with a modern building.

A FAMOUS LANDMARK OR BUILDING Next time you visit a famous landmark, aim to take one photograph that features the subject as it has been represented thousands of times before – on postcards, for example – and for the second, try to ring the changes by taking a shot from an unusual angle or level.

■ Visit the same location more than once as you're bound to spot details that you missed on previous trips.

■ If you want to photograph a famous landmark, arrive early in the morning when there are fewer people about.

WIDE-ANGLE/TELEPHOTO COMPARISON OF BUILDINGS This is a project for owners of zoom compacts. Photograph a group of buildings – this could be a small village in the hills or skyscrapers in a cityscape – with the wide-angle and telephoto extremes of your zoom lens. The aim is to produce a wide-angle picture showing the architecture set against an attractive backdrop, and a telephoto shot showing the effects of perspective compression.

INTERIOR WITH AMBIENT LIGHT Take a picture of the interior of a building using available lighting only – in other words you will need to switch the flash off. The most important thing is to produce an atmospheric shot that is free from camera shake. Remember that if the room is lit by sunlight, the results will appear natural, while artificial light may exhibit a colour cast.

YOUR HOME You may have lived in your home for years but when was the last time you took a picture of it? The final project involves taking creative photographs of the interior and exterior of your own home. Think how you can make the most of lighting, composition and viewpoint to bring out the character of your home. ■

⌒ The interior of the World Trade Center in New York has produced a pleasing composition, with the straight lines of the trees and pillars combining with the circular pattern in the foreground and the arches of the roof and window.

⊂ With a little creativity even a relatively nondescript building can be worth photographing. There is nothing particularly special about this balcony, but by tilting the camera forty-five degrees and making sure the image is framed by a stunning backdrop of blue sky, the result is a more exciting abstract shot.

Q&A: Architecture

I photographed a building and it appears on the photo as if it narrows toward the top. Why?

Take a photo of a building with the camera pointing upward and the building appears to be leaning backward. This effect is known as converging verticals. One way to avoid this happening is to stand farther back and keep the camera pointing straight ahead rather than tilted up. Alternatively, raise your viewpoint by standing on a wall or bench or by shooting from the upper floor of a building opposite to the one you want to photograph. However, the effect of converging verticals works really well when you want to illustrate the height of very tall buildings such as skyscrapers.

Any tips for shooting interiors?

If you're indoors, a wide-angle lens will fit more of the room in the frame. Use a flash if the interior is lit by artificial lighting, otherwise your pictures will have a colour cast.

Mount the camera on a tripod if you think the light is low enough to cause camera shake. If there's a mirror, include it in the frame to make the room look bigger, but make sure your reflection doesn't appear in the shot. If the room is particularly small, shoot from outside the room through a window or doorway.

Stained-glass windows

The interior of a church or cathedral can offer a number of photogenic delights, not least if there are some stained-glass windows on view. This is a fairly easy and accessible subject to get to grips with, and will bring a welcome boost of colour to any photo album.

Usually depicting religious characters or a biblical story, and combining intricate designs and bold colours, stained-glass windows are designed to show off the colours of the glass when light passes through it, so you will need to be inside to appreciate them.

Although the most common method for composing the window within the frame is to use a zoom facility, you should also aim to photograph the glass from different viewpoints. Shooting the window straight on is an obvious option,

but you should also experiment with unusual angles. Try getting close to the window and shoot upward at an acute angle or, if there is a balcony or raised area, do the same but with the camera pointing down. You should also try to take pictures of the entire window as well as moving closer or zooming the lens to

↻ For a different approach get close to the stained-glass window and take a picture of it from a very narrow angle. This has the effect of compressing the image and producing a more dramatic effect.

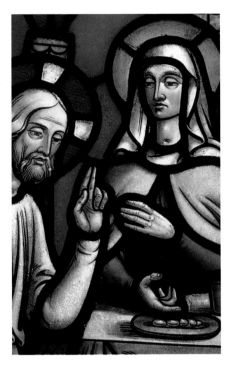

‌◔ Take care with the composition of your picture and make sure you include a good mix of colours. Here the scene has been carefully framed to include the two figures and the dish on the table.

↻ This is an example of a typical stained-glass window depicting a biblical story. Note the very intricate detail and excellent range of colours. Like many large windows, there is a black panel across its centre, but the many colours of glass camouflage it and prevent it being a major distraction.

focus on one pleasing detail such as a figure, a pattern or an eye-catching combination of colours. If the window is describing a well-known biblical story, try to extract some of the key scenes with your camera.

Don't be afraid to include some of the surroundings in the picture. Often the stained glass will be set into an arch, providing a natural frame for the shot. Sometimes a window will be framed by ornate pillars or gold leaf which can add extra interest to the image.

When you visit a church or cathedral, always seek out a member of staff and ask permission before you start taking

photographs. This way you might also learn a little more about the history of the stained glass, or find out if there are any interesting windows tucked away in areas of the building not usually open to the public. You should also find out in advance when services take place, so you can avoid these times.

Camera

Any type of camera can be used. A compact with a wide-angle lens is useful if the window is particularly large. However, a camera with a zoom lens is more convenient as it will make it easier to fill the frame with the window or zoom

in tight onto a particular part of the scene. If you are photographing a small area of the window, try to exclude the thin window frames as these can detract from the overall effect.

Film

To make the most of the glass's bright colours, use as slow a speed film as possible. For an inexpensive compact a medium-speed (ISO 100) film is recommended, but if you own a fairly expensive compact it's worth trying out a slow-speed film (ISO 50 or ISO 64). Print film will produce excellent results, but for more saturated colours it's worth using slide film.

Exposure

Most churches do not allow flash photography so you will need to switch the flash off. This isn't a major concern, however, as the glass would reflect the light from the flash and produce a hot spot on the picture. You should be fine hand-holding the camera, but if the light

↷ Some stained-glass windows are set into an arch which provides the perfect frame. When the light pours through the window at the correct angle you will find the arch emblazoned with the many colours of the glass.

shining through the window is particularly dim, or you're using a slow-speed film, you would probably be better off mounting the camera on a tripod.

The type of light shining through the glass will dramatically affect the quality of the result. Bright, direct sunlight will bleach the lighter colours in the glass and increase the contrast of the image. The best time to shoot stained-glass windows is on an overcast day when the lighting is more diffuse. This will provide a more even illumination and bring out the colours in the glass.

Many photographers worry that the light shining through the glass will cause the camera to underexpose the picture but this isn't the case. Most stained-glass windows have an equal amount of bright and dark tones so the camera's exposure is usually accurate.

↷ As well as photographing the entire window, try to isolate some of the intricate details by moving closer or zooming in the lens. This will enable you to take various shots of the same window.

PROJECTS

When was the last time you visited a church? Now here's another reason to go. Find a church or cathedral with a good variety of stained-glass windows and take five pictures. Two pictures should be of the same window, with one showing the entire window and the other focusing on a detail of it. ■

Q&A: Stained-glass windows

Should I worry about my reflection appearing in the picture?

Reflections aren't a major problem with stained-glass windows. If you notice your reflection in the glass, position yourself at a slight angle to the window.

Will the camera's autofocus system have any problem focusing on the stained glass?

No. Although autofocus systems encounter difficulties with clear glass windows, the multi-coloured panels in stained glass are easier for them to lock onto. However, if you do find that your camera's autofocus is having trouble locking onto the window, position the centre of the viewfinder on a part of the window that has several different colours. This will make it easier for the lens to focus.

Night scenes

A photographer's day doesn't have to end when the sun disappears. There are plenty of opportunities to take stunning after-dark shots, and various techniques to try out. So while others are tucked up in bed, why not spend a few hours practising your night-time photography.

FIREWORKS

Colourful pyrotechnic displays are popular at festivals and celebrations all around the world. In the UK, one of the best times to see fireworks is on Guy Fawkes' Night on the 5th of November, when the night sky is lit up with explosions of colour. Because firework displays are not generally commonplace events, you won't have much opportunity to practise your technique. However, it's true to say that getting great firework pictures is only 30 per cent technique; the other 70 per cent is in the preparation.

You should aim to arrive at the venue early so that you can take a position with an unobstructed view of the display. Set up your camera on a tripod so that it is pointing toward the sky. If the camera has a zoom, set it to the wide-angle setting as this will enable you to pick up the trail of the firework. If your camera features an infinity mode, use it to prevent any problems with the focusing system.

Once the firework display begins, look through the viewfinder to make sure that the explosions are included in the frame and make any necessary adjustments. All you then need to do is fire the shutter when you see the fireworks rising in the sky. This should record the trail and the explosion. If you are using the Bulb mode, keep the shutter open for several explosions as this will produce a more dramatic result. For a couple of the shots, it's always a good idea to include some of the crowd in the frame. This will not only give a sense of scale to the images but will also result in an attractive series of silhouettes.

◐ As this shot shows, including some of the crowd at the bottom of the frame can help add scale to the explosions.

○ An exposure of around eight seconds was enough to record a series of fireworks exploding to produce this colourful shot.

⊃ After a few minutes it should be possible to work out the height that various fireworks travel before exploding. By carefully zooming the lens, you will then be able to fill the frame with fireworks exploding at different heights.

Camera

Because you will want to include a large amount of sky in the frame, a camera (including zoom compacts) with a wide-angle lens of around 28mm or 38mm is ideal. The need for long exposure times means that many digital cameras and some compacts are not suitable.

Film

Colour film is a must as the main impact of the image will rely on the dramatic explosions of colour. ISO 100 slide film is recommended as it will make the most of the many colours on display.

Exposure

Switch the flash off to ensure a slow shutter speed. Select the Bulb setting if available; this will keep the shutter open for as long as you want, giving you more control over the exposure. Because of the long shutter speeds, a tripod is essential to avoid camera shake.

FLOODLIT BUILDINGS

Towns and cities take on a completely different look at night, not least because some buildings are floodlit in a range of colours. A building with a drab, grey exterior by day can be transformed by artificial light at night. Floodlit buildings are often places of importance, such as cathedrals, churches and landmarks, but other good subjects for night-time photography may include a city's financial centre, a theatre or an art gallery.

Artificial lighting usually produces a warm orange colour on standard colour film and this often combines with coloured floodlights to produce some interesting results.

Buildings next to water often make good subjects for floodlit photography, the reflections from the surface adding an extra dimension to the image.

Camera

Any camera is suitable as long as it allows long shutter speeds of at least a few seconds. A wide-angle lens is ideal for fitting an entire building into the frame or for including reflections, but a zoom offers more scope for composition.

Film

Use an ISO 100 colour print or slide film.

Exposure

Set the camera on a tripod and switch the flash to the off position to enable long exposures. If the camera has exposure compensation, add between +1 or +2 stops. A Bulb mode is perfect. If your camera has this facility, use it and take a series of exposures ranging from five to thirty seconds to ensure that at least one frame is properly exposed.

☾ At night, Tower Bridge in London is floodlit by several powerful tungsten lights. This shot was taken at the wide-angle end of a zoom with the camera on a tripod and set to its Bulb mode. Shooting at an angle leads the viewer into the image from the higher front tower on the left.

↷ Walking onto the bridge and using the telephoto end of the zoom has produced a very different result. Tilting the camera and picking out details in the architecture has resulted in an abstract shot.

➲ There was still enough light in the sky to enable the photographer to take this shot of New York's Chrysler Building without a tripod.

Top tip
■ Shooting shortly after sunset will mean that detail and colour in the sky will be recorded on the film.

FUNFAIRS

As well as providing entertainment for all the family, funfairs offer great scope for exciting night-time pictures. The combination of bright flashing lights set against a backdrop of pitch-black sky and the fast speeds of some of the rides can produce some dramatic photography.

Long exposure times will result in the lights on the fast-moving fairground rides appearing as a series of multicoloured streaks. Try to incorporate the whole scene in one or two shots and then focus on individual rides. It is also worth taking pictures while the rides are stationary as well as when they are moving. And remember to include people having fun in some of the shots.

As a precautionary measure, keep an eye on your camera at all times and make sure you set up your tripod in a position where it is not likely to be knocked over and damaged by people getting on and off the rides.

Camera

Most cameras are suitable for this kind of photography as decent results can be achieved with exposure times as short as one second. A wide-angle lens will allow you to get fairly close to the rides and produce a strong composition.

Film

Use colour film to record the bright colours of the fairground lights. An ISO 100 print or slide film is ideal. Because the subjects are lit by artificial lighting, it's worth opting for a film that produces vivid colours.

Exposure

Mount the camera on a tripod and switch the flash to the off position to produce some long exposures.

If your camera has a Bulb facility then use it and vary the exposures from around one second to about 30 seconds

↻ ↺ Varying the exposure time produces very different effects. In this set of fairground pictures, everything has remained constant apart from the exposure time. The camera was mounted on a tripod and the Bulb mode was switched on. The first shot was taken with an exposure of around one second (below left), the second shot with an exposure of approximately three seconds (below).

⌒ For this third shot in the series, an exposure time of around ten seconds has resulted in a smoother and fuller series of streaks. Despite the longer exposure time, the sky remains pitch black.

Top tips

■ If your camera comes with an infrared remote control, use it to take the picture rather than pressing the shutter button as this reduces the risk of camera shake.

■ After taking a few shots, vary the camera position to produce a slightly different result.

to create different results. The longer the exposure, the more streaks will appear in the photograph. The length of the exposure often depends on the speed of the ride. A slow-moving subject requires a relatively long exposure time to produce a series of colourful streaks. With a fast-moving ride, however, you can produce a striking image with an exposure time of only a few seconds.

PROJECTS

Be prepared to spend a few nights out under the stars to complete the following projects. Bear in mind that you won't get many opportunities each year to take pictures of fireworks or funfairs so make sure you are ready.

FIREWORKS Produce a series of four firework photographs. Each should show a different result. Try varying the exposure times and also use the zoom, if your camera has one, to record the fireworks' trails. Make sure that one or two of the shots feature members of the crowd to provide a sense of scale.

FLOODLIT BUILDINGS Take your tripod into town and take photographs of four floodlit buildings. You should include a number of light sources, such as tungsten and halogen, and experiment with different focal lengths if your camera has a zoom. One of the shots should show a waterside setting, with the lights of a bridge or building reflecting in the water.

Once you have completed this, choose your favourite building, revisit it and take another two pictures, this time from differing viewpoints.

FUNFAIRS The next time a funfair visits your local area, pop along and produce a set of three pictures, each showing a different ride. Vary the exposure times to achieve a series of effects. Try and do this project on the opening day as it will allow you plenty of time to return if you don't get the results you are looking for. ∎

↻ ↺ This comparison set shows the same ride before and after it started to move. The exposure time for both shots was around ten seconds.

Q&A: Night scenes

When is the best time to take pictures?
You will usually find that the two or three hours after the sun has set is the best time. This is because there is still some light in the sky meaning detail can be recorded. However, a pitch-black sky provides a dramatic backdrop for colourful night-time scenes such as firework displays and funfairs.

Any general tips for night-time photography?
Wrap up warm if you're taking pictures in winter and carry a torch with you as it will help you to see what you are doing. Remember that personal safety should always come first. If you are shooting near a busy road, wear a reflective strip or brightly coloured top. If possible, try not to wander around on your own and carry a mobile phone or some loose change in case you need to contact somebody.

What's the best type of tripod for night-time photography?
Make sure that the tripod is sturdy enough to keep the camera completely steady. Also check that the head of the tripod is versatile enough for the camera to be tilted at various angles to allow you to take pictures from unusual viewpoints.

Sunsets

Few things in nature can rival the sight of a breathtaking sunset, when the entire sky is diffused with golden colour. Sunsets make beautiful subjects for photography and they are actually fairly easy to capture, so long as you are ready to work fast.

Good preparation is essential to taking exciting sunset shots. Check a local newspaper or contact a meteorological centre to find out the approximate times for the sunset in your area. Arrive early at your location and find a suitable position. Remember that if you are inland the sun will sink behind any hills or landmarks earlier than the stated time.

Some of the best sunset pictures include water, which reflects the sun's colours and adds to the photo's impact.

So visit the coast if you live nearby, or check a map of your region and locate your nearest large lake.

The weather can have a dramatic effect on the intensity and colours of a sunset. In overcast conditions it is often the case that no light penetrates the cloud cover,

↻ Boats look very photogenic set against a sunset backdrop. Here the soft colours of the sea and sky help to evoke a particularly romantic atmosphere. The exposure, taken from part of the sky, is spot-on, with good colours and detail in the boat and jetty.

☾ Don't be put off photographing sunsets because they lack the range of dazzling golden colours you were hoping for. The silhouette of this leaning palm tree dominates much of the frame and sits nicely against the blue sky. Positioning the horizon along the bottom third of the frame adds scale and contrast to the scene.

so sunsets are not dramatic. At the other end of the meteorological scale, a completely cloudless sky can result in a rather bland and unattractive sunset.

Some of the most atmospheric sunset photographs are taken when there are clouds in the sky, reflecting the sun's colours to produce a striking display of yellow, orange and red tones.

Flare can be quite a common problem when the sun is at such a low height, but you can reduce the risk of this appearing by excluding the sun from the frame.

You should also think carefully about the composition of the scene. With a multicoloured sky you may want to fill the frame entirely with sky and eliminate the land from the image. Another effective approach is to include silhouettes of some interesting foreground details, such as trees or boats, to add some scale and lead the eye into the picture.

If you are presented with a glorious sunset but lack suitable foreground detail, a silhouette of another person will add an extra element to the photograph. If you're on your own, mount the camera on a tripod, set the self-timer and put yourself in the frame.

Experiment with a variety of viewpoints and you will find that one sunset can produce many different images. Also, because it's the colours in the sky that you are trying to record, it's not always necessary to include the sun in the frame, so keep taking pictures as the sun disappears below the horizon. The sun sinks at an incredible rate, however, so you'll need to work fast. Use this time to take a series of shots, each with slight

↷ The silhouettes of two solitary trees help to draw the eye towards this magnificent flaming sky over the Masai Mara Game Reserve in Kenya.

differences in composition. Include foreground detail in some shots, while in others fill the frame with sky. This will provide you with a variety of images from one evening's work.

Camera

A zoom compact offers you the versatility to frame the image to suit the scene. Use a wide-angle setting to include plenty of foreground detail and sky, or zoom in close to make the sun larger in the frame. You will find a camera's spot-metering facility extremely useful.

Metering for sunsets

Imagine it. You're witnessing the most beautiful sunset you have ever seen, but you aren't sure how to meter for it. By the time you've worked out what to do, the moment has gone. Take a look at these three pictures. They were taken only seconds apart but a spot-meter reading was taken from different parts of the frame to produce three very different exposures.

SUNSET A
With a spot reading taken from the shadow of one of the boats the camera has overexposed the picture, resulting in the colours of the sky being bleached out.

SUNSET B
This shot is underexposed because a spot reading was taken from the sun at the centre of the frame. This has forced the camera to select too fast a shutter speed, resulting in a dark image.

SUNSET C
Taking a spot reading from an area of sky to the far right of the frame has produced the best exposure. There is plenty of colour in the sky and some detail on the boats is visible.

Film

Use a punchy colour film to make the most of the golden hues. Colour slide film has the most impact but you'll need to be accurate with the exposures. Start off with colour print film as it is easier to get good results with, then try out slides when you've gained more experience.

Exposure

Due to the brightness of sunsets, there is always the risk of underexposing the picture. Depending on the type of metering systems your camera uses, there are different methods for exposing the scene. If your camera has a spot facility, take an exposure reading from a mid-tone area, in other words part of the scene that isn't too light or too dark. This should result in good colour saturation of the all-important sky.

If your camera doesn't have this facility, there is an alternative. Your camera's metering (and focusing) systems are activated when you partly depress the shutter button. Take two shots, the first by locking the AF and metering with the camera pointing at the sky, then recomposing, the second by repeating this process but with the camera pointing at the foreground. This will produce two very different exposures, one of which should be correctly exposed.

Remember to switch the autoflash off as the flash isn't required. Also, if you

☞ Clouds can often make or break a sunset shot. The impact of this shot comes from the multitude of textures and colours produced by the interesting cloud formation in this dazzling sky. Including a small amount of foreground detail has added some scale without distracting from the sky.

have the zoom set at its telephoto end, you might want to place the camera on a monopod or tripod to reduce the risk of camera shake.

PROJECTS

Prove you don't need to visit exotic sun-drenched locations to capture beautiful images by taking three sunset pictures in your native country. At least one shot should be taken by the sea and include one or two foreground details. Remember that a colourful evening sky can create a dramatic and atmospheric backdrop for even the most mundane subjects, so keep a look out for unusual features on the landscape, the silhouette of a derelict building, perhaps, or an electricity pylon,

which might not be considered photogenic in daylight conditions.

The next time you go abroad on holiday, take pictures of another two sunsets. Try to encapsulate the atmosphere of the setting by featuring one or two foreground details, such as palm trees, so that the pictures contrast with those you took at home. ∎

Top tip
- Never look directly at the sun, either with the naked eye or through a viewfinder, as you could cause permanent damage to the eye.

Q&A: Sunsets

I've had my sunset prints returned and the sky lacks the gorgeous orange colours I remember. Why?

Automatic printing machines are set up to deal with average conditions and may have problems with certain subjects, including sunsets. This means they sometimes print the pictures with the wrong exposure – making it too light or dark, or with the wrong colour – replacing the vivid orange with a more neutral shade.

What can I do about it?

Return any prints you're not happy with, along with the negatives, to your lab and explain that the pictures are of sunsets. You should find that the reprints will show the colours you expected. Another option is to use slide film and then have a print made from the slide you are happiest with.

What sort of subject should I include in the foreground?

Anything that adds interest to the scene. If your sunset is taken on a beach, include a palm tree or a pier. If you're including water in the scene, then boats are a good choice.

Won't they be underexposed?

Not necessarily, but don't worry if this does happen. An underexposed foreground subject, appearing as a silhouette against the bright colours of the sky, can enhance the picture.

ᴖ Sometimes it pays to fit the main subject in the middle of the frame. This scene shows the sun beginning to drop below the horizon. It's a fairly monotone image, with very little colour in the sky or foreground, but the silhouettes of the people on the beach and the colours of the orb produce a pleasing composition.

ᴄ The success of this image lies in the interesting foreground detail rather than in the actual sunset itself. The tall masts of the boats on the left and right draw the eye in toward the centre of the frame. A waving figure beside the small boat at the end of the jetty adds some human interest to what otherwise would have been an ordinary sunset shot.

Silhouettes

This type of photography is all about drawing the viewer's attention to the outline of a subject rather than to the details. By underexposing your subjects and positioning them in front of a bright background you can create some intriguing and dramatic effects.

You might think it something of a contradiction in terms to be offered advice on how you can grossly underexpose your subjects. After all, camera manufacturers have invested millions in developing metering systems that help you to set the correct exposure. However, silhouette photography lends itself to a variety of subjects, from people to landscapes, and can result in some fascinating shots.

The basic idea is to underexpose the subject so that it appears as a solid black outline against a lighter background. The subjects that lend themselves best to this treatment are those that are instantly recognizable – people or trees, for instance. You will need to shoot against a bright background; a large expanse of water – the sea or a lake – is ideal as the surface reflects the sunlight. Alternatively you can shoot objects against a bright sky. If you live near an airport, for instance, it is well worth visiting in the early hours of the morning or in the evening when the colours in the sky make an exciting backdrop for the outlines of the low-flying planes.

The secret to successful silhouette photography is to make sure that the subject is positioned directly between you and the background. Very bright backlighting will result in a solid black, almost two-dimensional outline. You should also ensure that the background isn't cluttered, as this will distract attention from the silhouette.

If the background lighting isn't overly bright, it is unlikely that your silhouette will be completely black. In these situations, some detail around the edges of the subject will be recorded, often enhancing the mood of the shot. Silhouettes of people work very well when there is less intense background lighting, because a rim of light around the hair can impart an attractive radiance to the shot.

If you come across a suitable subject for a silhouette photograph – perhaps the outline of a sailing ship at sea or a well-known building – but find that the light source is not directly behind or that the background is cluttered, try looking at it from another position.

Top tips

- If your camera has a spot facility, take a reading from the highlight to guarantee major underexposure of the subject.

- Make sure that you switch the camera's flash to the off position to prevent it from firing.

↻ A zoom lens was used to magnify this man paddling in the distance. The bright highlights of the sun reflecting on the water have fooled the camera into underexposing the subject, resulting in a pleasing silhouette.

↻ Bonfires are a good place to practise your silhouette photography. Look out for someone standing between you and the bonfire and snap away. In this case, a young child on an adult's shoulders provided an ideal opportunity.

Camera

Any type of camera is suitable but a zoom model will allow you to isolate the subject against the background.

Film

Any speed of film is suitable. Both colour and black-and-white film can be used, although results are often more dramatic with the former. Slide and print films are both acceptable but if you do use print film, you may find that the processor has tried to counteract the effect of the silhouette. If this happens, have the frame reprinted and explain what you were trying to achieve.

Exposure

To produce a silhouette, the subject must be underexposed. If most of the frame is filled by a bright background, the metering system of most cameras will expose for this and automatically underexpose the foreground subject.

PROJECT

Take two people silhouettes. Remember that the outline of the subject should be clearly evident. Once you've mastered this technique, aim to produce an interesting silhouette of an easily identifiable object such as an umbrella, a shoe or a candlestick. ■

☝ A simple, uncluttered composition is a key element of a good silhouette shot. Here the interesting shapes of the streetlight, the tree and the distant building occupy only a small part of the frame but create a dramatic effect. Including the bright sun in the frame adds contrast to the scene.

☝ Water can provide the ideal setting for exciting silhouettes. In this ethereal seascape, a fishing boat provides foreground interest, its dark outline contrasting well with the light reflections of the water, while the distant hills make a good backdrop.

Q&A: Silhouettes

How should I frame the silhouetted subject?

The cleaner and brighter the background, the better the image will be. Ideally, you want to have the subject positioned in front of a clean sky or expanse of water, so that it stands out and doesn't merge with other elements in the frame.

What subjects make good silhouettes?

Anything with a recognizable shape, even though no detail is visible, makes a good silhouette. If you have a willing friend it is easy to set up a silhouette shot – all you need do is position them against a bright background and snap away. Cyclists make good subjects as their outlines are easily identifiable. Silhouettes of windsurfers work well as the shape of the sail produces an abstract result.

Is there anything I should be aware of when taking outdoor silhouettes?

Keep an eye out for flare from the sun. Avoid the problem by keeping the sun out of the frame or by obscuring it behind a tree or other large object.

Can I take silhouettes indoors?

Yes. Small objects such as bottles or ornaments can make good silhouette photographs. An open fire makes an ideal backdrop or you can position your subject in front of a window.

Patterns

Repetition doesn't have to be monotonous, especially if you're a photographer on the look out for exciting patterns. Take a little time to look around and you will discover that the world is full of interesting patterns waiting to be photographed.

Including some elements of pattern in a photograph can help to bring a visual order and balance to the composition – a formation of rocks in a pool, say, or the serried rows of spectators at a football match. A repetition of lines, colours, textures or shapes can also be used to create abstract images.

You can find inspiration for eye-catching patterns everywhere. Take a stroll in the countryside and they will appear in a field full of flowers, in the furrows of a ploughed field or in an arrangement of autumnal leaves on the ground; walk around town and patterns will emerge in cars, columns, rooftops, windows, bricks or pillars.

With a little imagination, even seemingly mundane objects can be transformed into interesting patterns. A set of coloured pencils placed side by side or a row of identical bottles are just some

of the everyday objects that you can use. You will often find patterns within patterns. If you're shooting a building with floor after floor of windows, for instance, look at how the individual panes create their own pattern.

Sometimes the repetition of different colours can be enough to create a good pattern photograph. You could focus on a section of brightly coloured clothing, for instance, or zoom in on the stripes of a zebra or the squares on a chessboard for a striking monochrome shot.

Camera

You can use any type of camera, but one with a zoom lens is preferable as it will make it easier to frame the pattern and eliminate everything else from the frame.

↻ These barrels were photographed in a Kentucky whisky distillery. Due to the cramped conditions, the lens was left in its wide-angle setting in order to fit in as much of the scene as possible. The camera was laid on the floor pointing upward and the self-timer was operated to allow the photographer to get out of the frame.

↻ Modern architecture can be a good source of patterns. The curved white balconies and black railings of this hotel in Florida were shot with a telephoto zoom at an angle to produce an eye-catching abstract pattern.

Top tip

■ Black-and-white film can bring a graphic quality to pattern pictures and is useful when you want to eliminate any distracting colours.

A close-up facility is worth having as it allows you to fill the frame with a small still life or isolate part of a larger subject.

Film
Colour film is ideal if your subject is made up of a variety of colours. But don't dismiss black-and-white film; the lack of colour can sometimes help the viewer to concentrate on the repetition of form and shape in the subject.

Exposure
Most patterns do not pose a problem for a camera's exposure system, so you should be confident of good results with the camera in fully automatic mode. However, for backlit shots or shiny subjects, use the spot-metering mode and meter from a mid-tone.

PROJECTS
INDOOR PATTERNS Take a picture of two different patterns that you have planned and set up yourself. Look for symmetrical subjects such as a group of bottles or a collection of books on a shelf.

ARCHITECTURAL PATTERNS Your aim is to produce four photographs that show

↻ The plumage of a male peacock makes a dazzling pattern subject. A zoom was used to fill the frame with the feathers, while keeping the bird's head in the centre and shooting straight onto the subject brings a pleasing uniformity to the shot.

clear patterns in the architecture of different buildings. You will find that some of the most pleasing subjects are composed of a series of curves and straight lines, so look out for features such as pillars, windows, arches and balconies and aim to incorporate a couple of these elements in one shot.

OUTDOOR PATTERNS Search your local area and find four subjects that will make good pattern shots. At least one of the subjects should be man-made, perhaps a row of cars shot from an interesting angle or colourful umbrellas in a crowd, while another should feature a pattern from nature such as a line of trees, an interesting rock formation or ripples on the surface of water. ■

ↄ A common enough sight, but this rear view of a row of bikes in Amsterdam makes an engaging black-and-white shot, with the juxtaposition of frames, saddles, handlebars and wheels forming an interesting pattern.

Top tips

- Shadows often produce their own patterns. You'll find that the best time for shadows is early or late in the day.

- When photographing small objects, try to keep the background as uncluttered as possible so as not to detract the viewer from the main focus of attention.

↝ Colours, lines and textures combine in this intricate pattern which is nothing more elaborate than tiling on a roof.

↻ Sunglasses placed at regular intervals on a large rack provided the inspiration for this abstract pattern shot. Zooming in to eliminate the edge of the rack, the camera was tilted at an angle to produce an interesting composition.

○ Homing in on a section of railway track has produced an eye-catching shot, with a dusting of snow giving definition to the tracks and sleepers. Although this may look like a black-and-white image, it was in fact taken with colour film.

↻ A sequence of bird footprints in the snow makes a simple but effective composition. Exposure compensation was required to prevent the snow from causing the shot to be underexposed.

Q&A: Patterns

What subjects make the best patterns?

Anything with symmetry or repetition is ideal. Look for patterns within a single object such as windows or pillars on a building. Alternatively, look for a series of objects that make up a pattern, such as bricks in a wall, books or parked cars.

What should I do if I can't find suitable subjects?

Create your own. All you need to do is group together a collection of identical objects and you have made your own pattern. Coins, flowers or bottles can all create pleasing and photogenic results.

Have you any ideas for producing abstract pattern pictures?

Successful abstract shots are those that concentrate on one part of an object or scene to isolate a pleasing combination of colours, shapes, textures or lines. You could use the close-up facility on your camera to photograph a dartboard, for example, homing in on part of the board to produce a picture that contains elements such as the circle of the bull's-eye, the straight lines of the wire separating the numbers and the alternating colours.

Special effects

Many compact cameras will enable you to create some weird and wonderful images. Although these special effects cannot be produced on a digital camera, most image-manipulation packages will allow you to re-create similar results.

Feeling creative? Then be adventurous and try out something fun and imaginative with these special effects.

TRAFFIC TRAILS

Think of traffic and images of delays, fumes and noise usually spring instantly to mind. It's probably never occurred to you that photographing traffic can result in some dazzling shots and it is a relatively easy technique to master. It's not the vehicles themselves that you're trying to photograph but the light from

the headlights and rear lights, and to do this you obviously need to shoot at night. The lights are captured as trails because a long exposure is used, therefore recording the journey of the vehicles during the exposure.

Major roads or motorways offer the most potential for exciting traffic trails because these have a high volume of traffic. Shooting in the centre of a busy town or city will provide a photogenic backdrop for the traffic trails, enabling you to include lights from the

⊃ Don't limit your traffic-trail photographs exclusively to the land. This long exposure shows the effect of a boat travelling down river.

⊂ This shot was taken through a window using the infinity lock feature and shows a traffic trail splitting the image across the centre of the frame.

surrounding buildings in the frame. Try to position yourself on a bridge or walkway overlooking the traffic so that you can include as much of the road as possible. If you live by a main road you could also shoot out of an open upstairs window.

Straight roads will produce good results but you will usually get more interesting effects with roads that have plenty of bends and curves in them. Even better, photograph junctions, such as crossroads or roundabouts, for a striking array of trails. If you live close to an airport, it's worth including a large amount of sky in the frame so you can record the light trails of aircraft set against the night sky. You can even use your camera to capture the trails of traffic on a river.

Camera
Any type of 35mm or APS compact camera is suitable as long as it offers a slow shutter speed of a few seconds or a Bulb facility. Cameras with a wide-angle lens are ideal as they will allow you to include a large area of the road. If you have a zoom compact, use it at its widest

setting. Make sure that the flash is switched to the off position.

Film
Any type of colour film can be used. A slow to medium speed will yield the best results and lead to a longer exposure. Slide film is preferable but if you do use print film, be sure to let your processing lab know you have photographed traffic trails, because the large area of night sky may cause exposure problems for the automated printing machines.

Exposure
Because of the long exposure times, a tripod is essential for this type of photography. Shooting shortly after the sun has set will enable you to record details in the night sky, while late at night the dark sky makes a dramatic backdrop for the bright trails of light. If your camera has a Bulb facility, vary the exposures from a few seconds to around half a minute. The longer the exposure, the more light trails will be recorded and the greater the distance they will cover.

BULB MODE

The Bulb mode is found on many compacts and provides plenty of scope for creative indoor or night-time shots. Using this feature opens the shutter until you decide the film has received enough exposure. Because of the long shutter speeds, a tripod is essential.

The method for opening and closing the shutter varies from camera to camera. With some models you need to keep the shutter depressed, because releasing it ends the exposure. The problem with this method is that if you accidentally move the camera during the exposure you could blur the result. A better option is the 'two press system'. You press the shutter button once to start the exposure, then press it again to end it. This method greatly reduces the risk of camera shake.

A better option still is to use a remote control to open and close the shutter. With this method the camera does not need to be touched at all so there is no risk of camera shake.

Camera

Check that your camera has a Bulb facility, usually depicted on the camera's LCD as a capital 'B'. Some cameras also offer a Bulb with flash mode, which fires the flash at the start of the exposure to illuminate any foreground detail.

Film

A medium-speed colour film will record plenty of detail and produce well-saturated colours.

Exposure

Because the light is so low in this type of

These three pictures were all taken in St Michael's Caves, Gibraltar, and help to illustrate the difference between using the camera's built-in flash and the Bulb mode.

◑ This first shot, taken with flash, has exposed the bottom of this pillar but the rest of the scene is outside the flash range, resulting in a dark and rather uninspiring image.

photography, even a second or two difference in exposure time might not produce any visible difference in the photograph. Therefore it's worth taking a series of exposures at four or five second intervals. For example, try taking the first Bulb exposure at around 5 seconds, the next at 10 seconds, then at 15 seconds and so on up to around 30 seconds.

The less light there is, the longer the exposure that is required, so in very low light you might need to give an exposure of one minute or more.

↻ Using the Bulb facility has produced a much better shot. This area of the cave was illuminated by a few scattered spotlights which meant that an exposure of around fifteen seconds was required. A tripod was not available, so the camera was supported on its soft case and placed on top of a litter bin. The tungsten lighting has given the photo a warm orange glow.

↻ A wide-angle lens was used to fit in a large area. The long exposure has captured some of the people walking around as a series of blurs, most prominent in the lower left corner.

COLOUR INFRARED FILM

Kodak's colour infrared 35mm film is unlike any other and can be used to create some spectacular effects. Whereas standard colour films are sensitive to the visible spectrum, that is visible colours, this specialist film is sensitive to the infrared end of the spectrum.

Kodak's colour infrared is one of the most expensive slide films on the market, but its unique characteristics make it one to try out if your camera has the necessary features.

Camera

Colour infrared film requires careful handling and its unique characteristics mean it can be used only in certain

compacts. To get the very best from this type of film, a colour filter needs to be attached to the lens. You also need to be able to adjust the exposure by changing the film speed or using exposure compensation. If your camera has these features then you should be able to get good results from infrared film.

Another point to bear in mind is that infrared radiation focuses at a different point in the visible spectrum to light. Using a wide-angle lens prevents this from being a problem due to the depth-of-field it produces. You can also increase depth-of-field by using a small aperture such as f/11 or f/16, assuming your camera allows you to adjust apertures.

Exposure

Colour infrared slide film is not DX-coded but should be rated at ISO 200. However, using colour filters reduces the amount of light reaching the film, so you should rate the film at ISO 50 by changing the film speed. The way the film records the image depends on the amount of infrared radiation; the sunnier the conditions, the more infrared radiation there is. For this reason, it is worth bracketing your exposures by two stops to ensure you get a good result.

Using different colour filters changes the colours the film records. Without a filter, the result has a very green cast and lacks a good range of colours. The best choice is a red filter, which records green foliage as deep reds and deepens the blues

☾ This eye-catching shot was taken with a red filter which has added dramatic hues to the blues of the sea and sky, and transformed the green foliage.

⌐ This coastal scene was photographed on Kodak EliteChrome slide film, which records an accurate range of colours.

⌐ Shot on Kodak infrared film, the image takes on a completely different perspective. The sea has become much bluer, while the trees in the background are now purple rather than green. Note, too, that the yellow buoy is now white, while the ship's red flag is yellow.

in sky and water. You should also experiment with orange and yellow filters.

Colour infrared film is very sensitive to light so it must be loaded in the dark. Once you have used the film, place it back inside the light-proof tub and have it processed as soon as possible. The film is processed in E-6 chemistry, which is standard for colour slide films. However, because it is less commonly used than other colour films, you should make sure the photo lab knows how to handle the film and give them instructions not to remove it from the tub in daylight, as this would ruin the film.

Top tip
- Some compacts, including all those with databacks, have an infrared sensor that fogs a small part of the film. Check with the camera manufacturer for details.

CROSS PROCESSING

All films are designed to be processed in a particular chemistry, with colour print films requiring the C-41 process and colour slide films E-6 chemistry. Cross processing involves processing films in the 'wrong' chemistry – colour print film in E-6 chemistry and colour slide film in C-41 chemistry – so your print film comes back as slides while your slide film is returned as negatives and prints.

There are a number of factors that will determine how the cross-processed prints or slides will appear. The film choice is the first factor. Every type of film will produce a different result, even films from the same range but with different speeds. Another factor is the processing itself, as minor variations in the temperature or the processing time can alter the result.

Cross processing print films usually requires a large drop in the film speed, in other words an ISO 200 film will give the best exposure when rated at ISO 50 or 100. This means that a camera with some sort of exposure control is handy. Slide films don't show such a large change, however, so if your camera doesn't have this facility, give slide films a go.

Camera

Any compact is suitable, but one with a film speed override or exposure compensation facility is preferable.

Film

Any type of colour film can be used. Try out a couple of brands and stick with the one you're happiest with.

Exposure

You will need to experiment to find out each film's best speed rating. If your camera has an ISO speed override or exposure compensation facility, bracket your exposure by around two stops. Cross processing slide films requires little or no exposure adjustment so use slide film (which will be returned as prints) if your camera lacks exposure control.

This set of comparison pictures shows the effects of cross processing slide and print film

↻ This shot was taken on colour slide film and processed in the proper chemistry to produce natural-looking colours.

☾ For this next shot, colour print film was processed in slide chemistry to produce a colour slide. ISO 100 Konica film was used and has resulted in a light brown colour cast, which is most noticeable in the sky. However, some of the colours, including that of the grass, are fairly accurate.

↻ The strong green cast and muted colours displayed in this print are the result of a slide film being cross processed to produce a set of negatives.

MULTIPLE EXPOSURES

This technique involves taking more than one exposure on the same frame and can result in some surreal shots. The most common type of multiple exposure is to photograph the same person twice on the frame, or to zoom in on the moon so that it looks unnaturally large in the frame and then expose it with a landscape. Once you have mastered the technique, you are limited only by your imagination.

Camera

A compact with a multiple exposure facility is ideal. Set this function and the camera will not wind on the film until two exposures have been taken.

It is possible to try out this technique if your camera lacks a multiple exposure

facility but it is a little more complicated. You will need to use the entire roll of film and then reload it back into the camera. So, if you want to superimpose the moon onto another image, for instance, you will need to photograph the moon on every frame and when you're ready to take the second shot, reload the film. With an APS film this means adjusting the status indicator from the number three setting (used but not processed) back to number one (unused) – see pages 22–29. For a 35mm film, use a film retriever (see page 74) to pull out the film from the cassette, then reload it.

Film

A medium to fast print film is the ideal choice, as its wide exposure latitude is able to handle errors in exposure much better than slide film.

Exposure

Getting the exposure right can be tricky. Position the first subject against a black background to ensure that it looks solid in the final result. If you shoot against a coloured background the subject will have a ghostly appearance because it will be superimposed on the background.

It is important to remember where the subject was positioned in the first set of exposures because you will need to make sure that in the second set it isn't in the same position, otherwise they will be superimposed on each other.

c Try to make sure that one of the subjects in the multiple exposure is colourful so that the two elements stand out against each other, as in this shot where brightly coloured flowers have been chosen as a backdrop for a portrait.

PROJECTS

The following projects will help you to develop your repertoire of special effects.

TRAFFIC TRAILS Take two pictures of traffic trails – one from a high viewpoint, the other from ground level. Remember to use long exposures to maximize the lengths of the trails.

BULB MODE Practise your Bulb photography by finding two suitably dark places to take pictures. Vary the length of the exposures and take notes. When you get the film developed you can check your notes to see which exposures gave the best results, making future Bulb exposures a little easier to predict.

COLOUR INFRARED FILM If you're lucky enough to own a camera that can make the most of infrared film, produce four pictures that show off its amazing effects. Aim to include plenty of sky and foliage in a couple of them and also try out some people pictures to show the weird effect the film has on skin tones.

CROSS PROCESSING Take a set of portraits on slide film and print film, then have them cross processed and compare the results. It's worth trying a number of subjects with different hair colour or skin tone to see how the results vary.

MULTIPLE EXPOSURES Aim to take two successful shots. Try to include the same person in the frame twice, or if you have a zoom lens experiment by adjusting it between shots to change the scale of the subjects in the frame. ∎

Q&A: Special effects

How will traffic lights appear in a traffic-trail picture?

If the exposure is long enough, all three colours (red, amber and green) on a set of traffic lights will appear.

How many individual pictures can be taken on a multiple exposure?

In theory, you could take as many as you want, but in practical terms two or three shots is usually the limit.

Does it cost more to have a colour infrared film processed compared to a normal colour slide film?

The Kodak infrared film is processed in the same E-6 chemistry as standard colour slide films, so processing costs should be the same.

Will my local lab cross process film?

Some labs do not like to cross process films as they believe it will contaminate the chemicals.

Can I take pictures with flash if I want to cross process the film?

Generally, the stronger the lighting, the more contrast there will be on the image, so flash photography and bright sunlight are ideal.

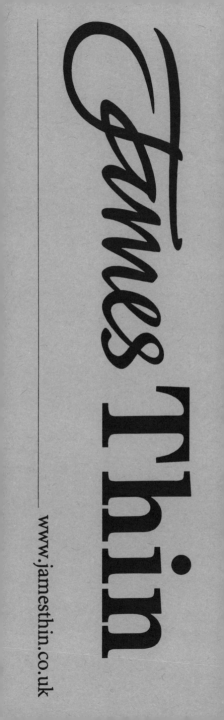

James Thin

www.jamesthin.co.uk

This is a little poem written by
James Thin (Jimmy, to his friends)
1923-1997

Where are you going?

(This is the most frequent question posed to the
trekker in Nepal, en passant - a damn silly question
really, as almost invariably there is only one place to
which one could possibly be going.
This is an attempt to answer the question.)

Where are you going? Nowhere, I said,
Up to the mountains to clear my head.

Why are you going? What does it matter,
Away from the world of bustle and clatter.

What will you do, when you get there?
I'll take a deep breath of wonderful air.

Why do you want to go so high?
To watch the clouds float over the sky.

Why are your feet so itchy to move?
For fear they stick in a mundane groove.

Why are you here, so far from the city?
Mortals below are worthy of pity.

Why can't you sit and enjoy the sun?
A lotus eater has little fun,

And man - if he really wants to survive -
Must always be doing, to stay alive.

Can you not be? Why must you do?
Why can't you sit and enjoy the view?

A man will rot if he stays quite still,
He must always see what's over the hill.

Won't you just wait and rest for a day?
Sorry, I can't, for I'm on my way.

Chapter Three

DIGITAL IMAGING

Digital cameras offer a myriad of opportunities for exciting, creative photography, and with the new generation of megapixel cameras, taking high-resolution pictures has never been easier or more affordable. Although you don't need to be a technological wizard to make the most of digital imaging, you will need to invest in one or two pieces of equipment, such as a computer and a printer. Focusing on the different types of hardware and software available, from scanners and removable hard disk drives to storage cards and printing paper, the following section will help you to decide exactly what is right for you. And even if you don't own a digital camera, you will see how you can still be part of the digital imaging revolution.

Hardware

This is the collective term used to describe all the equipment – including the computer itself and peripherals such as printers and scanners – that you will need to consider in order to untap the full creative potential of digital photography.

Setting yourself up for digital imaging can be expensive, so it's essential that you choose the right equipment and avoid any costly mistakes. As well as looking at the important factors to consider when buying a computer, this section also covers the important accessories (also known as peripherals) that you will need to begin your digital imaging adventure. These include the major types of colour printers, scanners for putting pictures taken with your APS and 35mm compacts onto the computer, and devices for increasing the memory capacity of your computer outfit.

A home computer is more than just a big grey box. A keyboard and mouse come as standard on most computers but you chould check the specification of the following components to make sure you get the best model for your requirements.

MONITOR

The screen size is the diagonal measurement from corner to corner. Most computers come supplied with a 14-inch or 15-inch monitor. However, the bigger the screen, the easier it is to view your image, so it's worth tying to upgrade it to a larger size, such as a 17-inch monitor or bigger. You should also ensure that the monitor has a high resolution screen and is able to display millions of colours.

COMPUTER HOUSING

This is the heart of the computer containing the main processor and the computer's memory. It is also where all the peripherals connect and where the disk and CD-ROM drives are found.

Processor

This is also known as the central processing unit, or CPU. Most PCs use a Pentium processor or equivalent. The faster the speed of the processor, the quicker it works, which is very important if you are working with graphics. The speed is measured in megahertz (MHz) and you should aim to buy a computer with a minimum speed of 166 or 200MHz. Keep an eye out for Pentium processors with MMX (MultiMedia eXtensions), a feature that helps the processor handle sound and graphics.

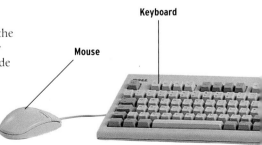

Keyboard

Mouse

RAM

This is an acronym for Random Access Memory, part of the computer's temporary memory where current files and programs in use are stored. The larger the RAM, the faster the computer can complete tasks and the larger the programs it can handle. Powerful image manipulation software uses up a lot of

FRONT VIEW

Computer checklist

Processing speed: Remember, the faster the better, so aim for at least 166MHz.

RAM: For digital imaging, look for a minimum of 32Mb.

Monitor: Opt for as big a screen as you can afford.

Hard drive: At least 1Gb is necessary if you want to load several software packages and store lots of images.

Ports and slots: Essential for connecting peripherals, so ensure the computer has at least two or three of each.

CD ROM: Look for at least a 12x model.

Monitor

Computer casing

On/off   Floppy disk drive   CD drive

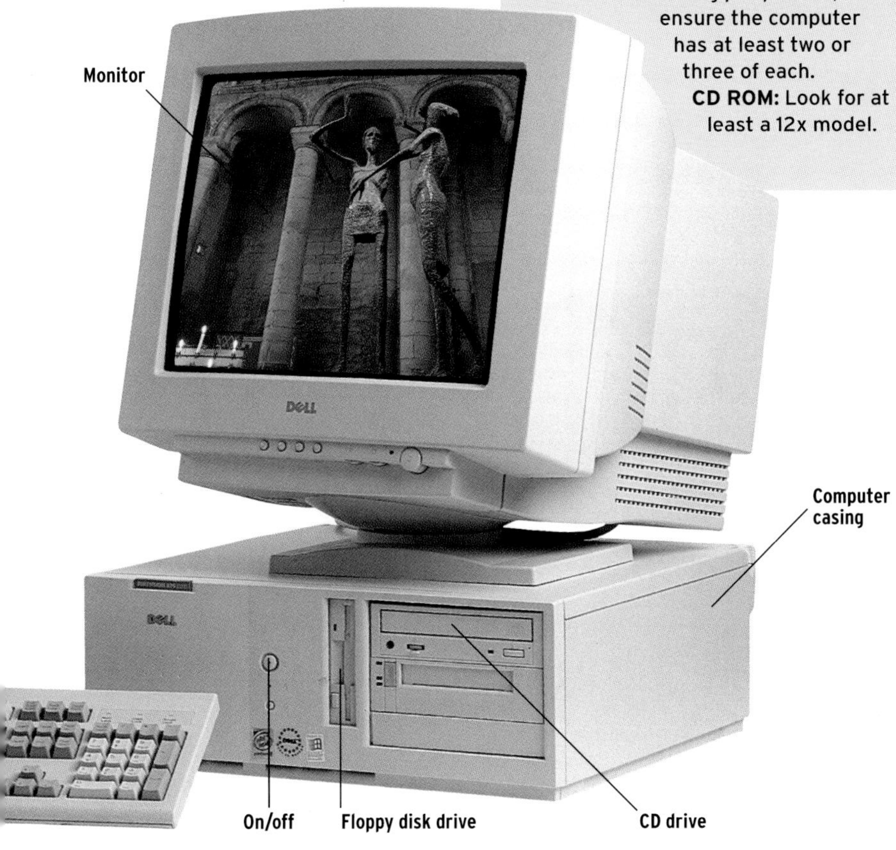

memory, so if you have only the minimum RAM requirements the computer may run slowly. To avoid this, opt for as much RAM as possible – 32Mb is useful but 64Mb is preferable. RAM is cheaper than ever before, so adding some extra memory is an affordable way of improving your computer's performance.

Hard drive

This is the filing cabinet of the computer. The higher the drive's capacity, the more programs and images it can store. Most computers offer hard drives with at least

1Gb, but if you're planning to store hundreds of images you should aim for at least 2Gb – even 6Gb is not excessive. It's also worth bearing in mind that some of the more powerful image manipulation software packages require a lot of storage space, so you will need a high-capacity hard drive.

Expansion slots

Inside the computer housing are sockets surrounded by empty spaces. These are expansion slots where you can add additional pieces of hardware in the

REAR VIEW

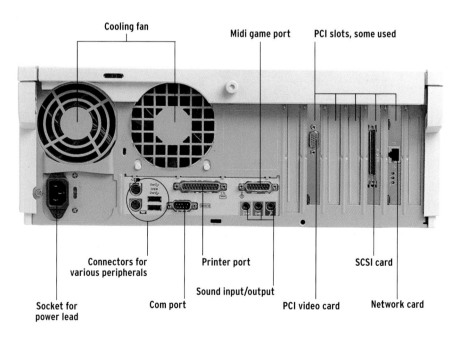

Cooling fan

Midi game port

PCI slots, some used

Connectors for various peripherals

Printer port

SCSI card

Sound input/output

Socket for power lead

Com port

PCI video card

Network card

future to upgrade your computer's performance. The current standard for PCs and Macs is the PCI (Peripheral Component Interconnect) expansion slot. Make sure your computer has at least two or three of these slots so that you will be able to make the most of any future developments in technology.

Ports
On the rear of the computer are sockets for the connection of extra peripherals such as printers and scanners. Check that your computer has more than enough of these ports for connecting all the peripherals you plan to use.

Graphics Card
The graphics card handles the colours. Look for a 24-bit card which can reproduce millions of colours. For image manipulation you should ensure that the card has at least 4Mb of video memory (VRAM).

Floppy disk drive
Used with almost all home computers,

floppy disks have been the standard way of transferring information for many years. However, their maximum capacity of 1.44Mb is suitable only for small files or low-resolution images. It's likely that in the next few years PCs will be produced without floppy disk drives.

CD-ROM drive
Most computers now come supplied with a CD-ROM (Compact Disk Read Only Memory) drive. This is set to remain the industry standard for a few years at least, as a CD can hold up to 650Mb of information. Most software packages now come supplied on compact disk. CD-ROM drives work at different speeds but you should aim for a 12x or 24x unit, which can rapidly access the information on the CD-ROM.

Some of the latest computers feature CD-ROM drives which offer a recording facility, enabling you to produce your own customized CD-ROMs. Some high-street photo labs also allow you to put pictures from your APS or 35mm film onto a CD-ROM at the processing stage. ∎

Apple Macintosh versus PC
The first major consideration is deciding which of the two main computer formats you should choose, the Apple Macintosh (Mac), or the IBM compatible personal computer (PC).

The Mac has always been the first choice of graphic designers and publishing houses due to its powerful graphics programs and user-friendliness.

However, PCs now offer similar software and the Windows system has made using them more user friendly. A big advantage of the PC is that there are a large number of manufacturers producing them, so there's an enormous variety of hardware and software to choose from. PCs also tend to cost less than similarly specified Macs.

Peripherals

This is the fancy word given to add-ons or accessories for your home computer. If you are serious about digital imaging then some peripherals, such as a printer or scanner, are essential. The following section will guide you through the choices.

THE PRINTER

Once you've played with your images on the computer, you will probably want to make prints of them. Home printers have become increasingly popular and are now more affordable than ever.

Inkjet printers and dye-sublimation printers are the most popular colour printers for home use. Two other types you may come across are dot matrix and laser. Dot matrix printers have very low resolution and are not suitable for producing prints. Laser printers are capable of exceptional quality but are prohibitively expensive for home printing.

Inkjet printers

These are the most popular as they are relatively inexpensive and produce high quality results. As the name suggests, this printer works by spraying tiny jets of ink onto the paper surface. Most printers use four colour inks (magenta, cyan, yellow and black), but some models also use light cyan and light magenta to produce a wider variety of colours.

Different manufacturers have their own methods for spraying the ink onto the paper. Epson, for instance, uses a piezoelectric method which controls the size and shape of the ink dot for very precise control. Other manufacturers, such as Canon and Lexmark, heat the ink before putting it onto the paper.

Dye-sublimation printers

This is a type of thermal printer offering higher print quality than an inkjet. This method of printing works by vaporizing dyes from a printer foil which are then absorbed by the printing paper.

These desktop machines tend to be more expensive than inkjets but will produce A6 colour prints of near-photographic quality. You must use special paper and ribbons, making this type of printer quite expensive to operate.

INKJET PRINTER

Paper tray

CHOOSING A PRINTER

You should consider the following factors before parting with your money.

Printer resolution

The resolution of a printer usually refers to the printer's ability to print a certain number of dots per square inch. Resolution is measured in vertical and horizontal dots per inch (dpi), for example 300x300dpi. As with the CCD of digital

Inkjet printer checklist

Resolution: Aim for at least a 600x600dpi model. For photo-realistic prints you will need a 1200x1200dpi model.

Printing speed: Make sure the printer isn't too slow or you could be waiting hours for your print to be produced.

Print size: Most print up to A4 size but if you want larger images, opt for a printer producing up to A3 prints.

Printing costs: Find out how much replacement ink cartridges and paper cost, as these can be expensive if you produce a lot of prints.

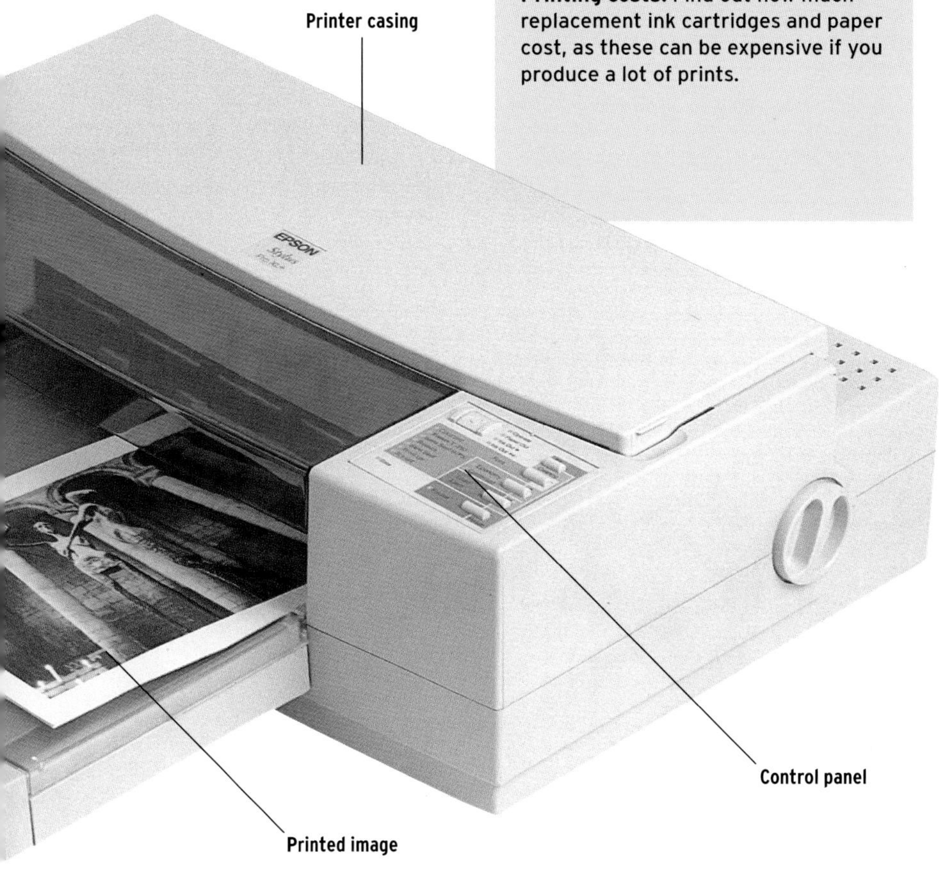

Printer casing

Control panel

Printed image

191

cameras, the higher the resolution, the better the quality. For printing text only, 300x300dpi is a high enough resolution, but for outputting photographs you should choose a model with as high a resolution as possible.

Printer speed

The speed at which a printer works is an often overlooked feature but a very important one. It's pointless using a printer with an extremely high resolution if it takes hours to produce a single print. The speed of a printer is measured in pages per minute (ppm); there are usually two ppm figures stated, one for producing black text and another for colour prints. It's worth looking at the printing speeds when you are trying to choose between printers with identical resolutions. You'll find that the latest printers now produce fast photo-realistic results.

Hidden costs

Bear in mind that you will need to replace the ink cartridges once they become empty. As you will find out, this can prove quite costly, especially if you are producing a large number of photo-quality prints, which use up more ink than lower resolution prints. Shop around for the best deal on ink cartridges; some outlets sell them at much cheaper prices than others.

Printer software

All printers come with the software needed to make them work correctly with the computer. As well as asking for a demonstration of the printer before you buy it, you should also ask to see the software in operation. Some are much more user-friendly than others, displaying useful information such as the remaining ink levels of the printer cartridges. ■

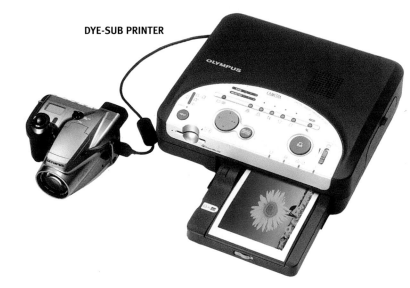

DYE-SUB PRINTER

Printing paper

Many papers are designed to work only with specific printers, so it's important to make the right choice. Some types of paper are completely incompatible with particular printers, resulting in problems ranging from the paper failing to pass through the printer, to the ink smudging and ruining the result.

One way of ensuring good results is to stick to the same brand as your printer, so choose Lexmark paper for a Lexmark printer and so on. However, there are many independent manufacturers producing superb papers. To find out which to choose, consult staff at your local dealer or consult buyers' guides in computer and photography magazines.

Most manufacturers produce a range of paper to suit different requirements. If you require a print of only average quality, then standard plain paper is suitable. However, the colours will lack vibrancy and the print will not have the sheen of a photograph.

For photo-realistic results you will need to use a photo-quality glossy paper or film. These are more expensive than other types of paper but can produce print-outs that are almost indistinguishable from those of conventional photographs in terms of resolution and colour reproduction. The packaging on the paper usually indicates the best resolution to set on the printer.

Another factor to consider is how long it takes for the ink on the paper to dry. Paper used in one printer might be dry to the touch in seconds, while the same paper used in another printer might take much longer to dry.

If you're feeling really creative, it's worth trying out textured papers or canvas/linen papers that produce prints with an 'arty' tapestry finish. These tend to be quite expensive but produce impressive results.

Some manufacturers produce starter packs with samples of different types of paper. Look out, too, for 'fun packs' containing adhesive paper for producing sticky photos and heat-transfer paper for printing your own T-shirts.

THE SCANNER

If you use a 35mm or APS compact camera and have hundreds of photographs, then a scanner gives you the chance to put your pictures onto the computer. Imagine the scanner as a mini photocopier, but rather than producing a paper copy, it creates a digital file. During scanning, a light is shone onto the image and sensors convert the picture into a digital form which can be stored and viewed on the computer.

Scanner resolution

As with printers, the resolution of a scanner is measured in dots per inch (dpi). If you want to reproduce high-quality results, scan at maximum resolution, but be aware that this usually results in very large file sizes that take up a lot of memory.

When setting the scanning resolution, you should work out what resolution and size you want the final print to be. An easy formula to follow is: *scanning resolution = final resolution x magnification*. For instance, if you want a 300dpi 12x8in print from a

6x4in print you must scan it at 600dpi (300dpi x2).

Types of scanner

There are two main types of scanner suitable for home use – the film scanner and the flatbed scanner.

FILM SCANNER This type of scanner can be used with 35mm colour and black-and-white negatives and slides. Many film scanners also come supplied with an adaptor for use with APS films. The strip of 35mm negatives or slides are placed in a holder which keeps them as flat as possible to ensure an accurate scan. With APS films, the cartridge is loaded into the holder, and the negative is automatically pulled out by the scanner.

Film scanners have a much higher resolution than flatbed scanners, with most offering a resolution of around 2700dpi. This is good enough to record very fine details from the negative or slide.

FLATBED SCANNER Flatbeds are cheaper than film scanners and are generally used to scan prints, rather than negatives or slides. The print is laid face down on the scanner and the lid is closed before the scan begins. Most scanners accept prints up to around A4 in size and can scan between 300–600dpi, although very expensive models scan at around 1200dpi. Some flatbeds accept optional hoods for scanning negatives or slides, but the resolution is nowhere near as good as from a film scanner.

Scanner software

The software that comes supplied with the scanner is usually fairly straightforward and easy to get to grips

FILM SCANNER

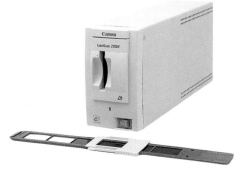

with. The usual procedure is to make a preview scan from which to make any final adjustments before making the final scan. Most software is TWAIN (Technology Without An Interesting Name) compatible, which means it will work with most major software packages.

Scanner speed

As with printers, the time taken for a scan to be made varies from model to model. Scan speeds can vary from one to six minutes depending on the scanner. You will usually find that the higher the scan resolution, the longer it takes. ■

Scanner checklist

Flatbed or film scanner: If you are working with prints, opt for a flatbed scanner. If you want to scan negatives or slides, choose a film scanner.
Film formats: Some scanners accept APS film as well as 35mm.
Software: Make sure the scanning software is easy to follow.
Scanner speed: Find out how long it takes for an image to be scanned, as times vary from model to model.

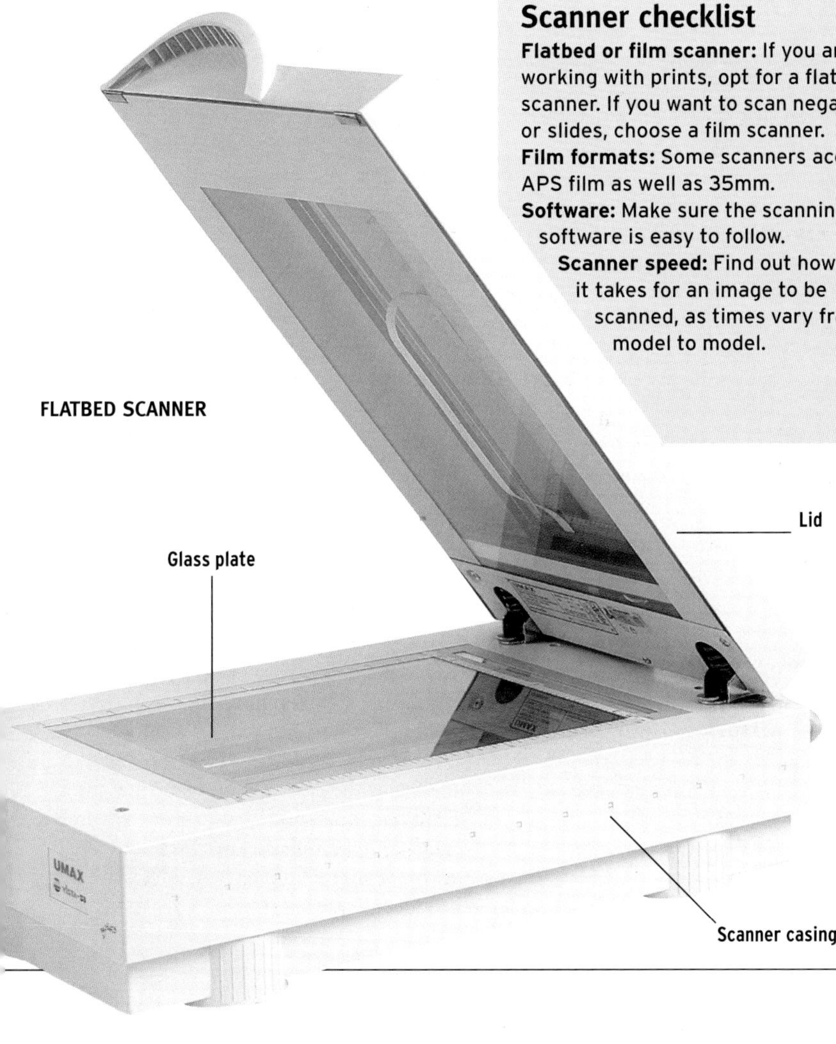

FLATBED SCANNER

Lid

Glass plate

Scanner casing

EXTERNAL STORAGE

Digital pictures take up a fair amount of hard-disk memory space, especially if they are high-resolution images. And if you have loaded any powerful computer software packages onto the hard disk, it may not be long before you notice a shortage of memory space. A way around this is to invest in some external storage. This acts like an additional hard disk, freeing up space on your computer. An external storage media is also useful for making a back-up of any important files or pictures in case your computer crashes and has its memory wiped. The main types of removable hard disks are:

Iomega Zip removable hard disk

This is one of the most widely used and cost-effective devices. In fact, the computer industry finds it so useful that many new computers come with a Zip drive fitted along with a floppy disk and CD ROM drive.

The Zip drive itself is cheaper than other types of external media and the relatively inexpensive Zip disks boast a very useful 100Mb capacity.

Iomega JAZ removable hard disk

This is a more expensive version of the Iomega Zip disk. The JAZ disk has a higher storage capacity of 1Gb so if you are going to store hundreds of high-resolution images the JAZ is a worthwhile option.

Rewritable CD-ROM drive

This accepts CD-ROMs onto which you can record information (known as CD-Rs). These drives, commonly known as CD writers, are becoming increasingly popular and are even found as standard on some top-of-the-range computers. Their appeal is that CD-Rs hold up to 650Mb of information and are extremely affordable. However, not all CD-ROM drives can read rewritable CD-Rs, so it is important to check compatibility before you invest in a CD writer.

There are two main types of rewritable CD-ROM. The most widely used allow you to write information onto them only once (CD-R). However, a recordable CD-ROM (CD-RW), although more expensive, has the advantage that you can erase as well as record data onto the disk.

Modem

Short for MOdulator-DEModulator, this is a device that connects your computer to the telephone line. A modem is essential if you want to use e-mail or be connected to the Internet, or if you want to use your computer as an electronic fax machine. Some computers come supplied with a built-in modem. Modems are available in different speeds: the faster they are, the quicker they can send or receive information. The speed is measured in kilobytes per second (Kbps) and you should aim for a model working at 56Kbps or more.

Storage card readers

The most common method of downloading pictures from your digital camera to the computer is by connecting the two with a cable. However, this can take some time and means that you are not able to use the computer until the pictures are transferred.

Storage card readers are becoming increasingly popular as they can transfer pictures incredibly quickly. They also allow pictures to be written onto a card from the computer. You simply pop the card into the slot and the reader's software automatically produces an on-screen menu so that you can view, download or erase any of the pictures on the card.

Many card readers are compatible with only one type of storage card but some, such as the ActionTec CameraConnect Pro, accepts the three major types of card (PCMCIA, CompactFlash and SmartMedia). ■

Q&A: Hardware

My computer has an SCSI socket. What is it for?

SCSI stands for Small Computer Systems Interface. It is a socket permitting a high speed transfer of information between the computer and a peripheral such as a scanner or external hard disk.

I've seen a 486 PC advertised at a very cheap price. Is it worth buying?

No. This is an earlier generation of computer and will not have enough power to handle current software. Save your money for a Pentium or equivalent machine.

At what resolution should I scan my prints?

For putting pictures on the Internet, a resolution of around 75dpi is high enough. For producing photo-quality prints, however, you should aim for around 300dpi.

Are all peripherals compatible with Macs and PCs?

No. Although some peripherals are supplied with the software to work with both, most will work only with one or the other. Check the compatibility before you buy.

How long does it take for a print from an inkjet printer to dry?

It depends on the printer and type of paper you use. With some printer/paper combinations the ink dries immediately, with others it can take hours.

Software

This is the collective term given to programs used by computers. To make the most of digital imaging you should consider carefully what software will be most appropriate for the image editing functions you have in mind.

If you want to play with your pictures and visually alter the image, then an image manipulation package could be the one for you. Depending on your requirements, this software will enable you to make simple modifications to your image, such as removing red eye or scratches, as well as create dazzling effects that would be difficult to achieve with conventional darkroom techniques.

However, if you want to build up a database of your pictures on the computer, then you will need an image cataloguing software package.

Fortunately, most current software packages usually offer both features, thus saving you money and the need to learn two different programs. Many also include the necessary files to produce your own web pages for the Internet without any need to learn complex procedures on setting up a website.

Software packages are extremely powerful and once you start using them, it's amazing what you can achieve. Some are easier to use than others, so if you're a complete beginner to digital imaging, make sure you don't buy anything too complex. Some manufacturers allow you to try out their software before buying it by supplying versions that work for only 30 days, or do not allow you to save the results. It's a good way of trying different 'shareware' packages.

SCREEN DISPLAY

Below is a typical screen display for a software package. Most are easy enough to find your way around quickly and many have very similar layouts, making

Toolbox   Menu bar

the switch from one package to another much easier.

MENU BAR This displays the main menu options. Clicking on the menu title with the mouse displays the menu options.

TOOLBOX With image manipulation programs, clicking on the various icons in this box selects a different tool which can be used to either alter, modify or enhance your digital image. Some of the more popular tools are discussed on the following page.

IMAGE WINDOW This is the part of the screen displaying the image. You can adjust the window's size to fill part or virtually all of the screen.

IMAGE MANIPULATION SOFTWARE

There is an enormous number of image manipulation software packages to choose from. They range from easy-to-use programs for removing red eye and retouching dust marks and sand scratches to extremely sophisticated packages that can be used to alter your digital image dramatically. The main functions of an image manipulation package are:

VIEWING Obviously it's impossible to work on an image if you can't see it, so the software must be able to display pictures from a digital camera or scanner. Most packages allow you to view several small images – known as thumbnails – on the screen at once.

RESIZING If your image is too big or too small you can adjust its size with this facility. Making an image larger usually results in a loss of quality.

Image window   Floating palette

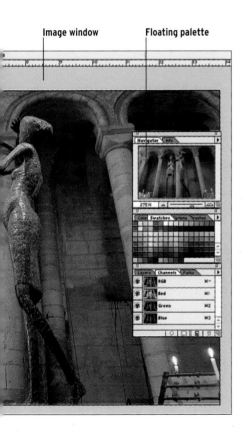

Shareware
Image manipulation software needn't be expensive. You can get shareware from magazines and the Internet. The programmers rely on your honesty to pay them a small fee if you decide to continue using it. You will also find that when you buy a computer, printer or another peripheral, you are supplied with image manipulation software as part of the package.

This is the name given to the program that allows other programs to work on the computer and is commonly known as an OS. On a PC the most common example is Microsoft Windows, while on an Apple Mac it's the Mac OS System.

ROTATION/FLIPPING You can use this command to rotate the image or flip it back to front. It is extremely useful if you have scanned in an image the wrong way round because it takes only seconds to correct the mistake, whereas rescanning the image can take minutes.

RETOUCHING This is a facility for removing scratches, dust or problems such as red eye from your picture. Retouching is one of the most commonly used features.

MIXING IMAGES It's easy to mix different images together to create a unique result. This is similar to producing a multiple exposure with a camera, but the effects possible on a computer could rarely be achieved with traditional methods.

ADJUSTING COLOUR AND CONTRAST You can change colour pictures to black and white, or create amazing colour images with black-and-white pictures. It's also possible to adjust the contrast of a picture to improve the result.

Tools for manipulation

These are the tools that you are most likely to use for manipulating images:
LASSO Also called the Freehand Mask in some software packages, this facility is used to select part of the image prior to it being manipulated. For instance, if you want to cut out a car to include in another picture, you would use this tool to outline the edge of the car.

MAGIC WAND This tool is used to select every area of a similar colour. You would use it, for instance, if you wanted to change the colour of the sky in one of your pictures. By placing the magic wand over part of the sky and clicking the mouse, all of the sky would be selected.

RUBBER STAMP Also known as the clone tool, this duplicates part of the scene and is useful for covering over unwanted objects in the shot. You can click on an area of sky, for instance, then paint this over something you want to remove such as a lamppost or electricity pylon.

TYPE This tool allows you to add text to your image.

ZOOM If you want to manipulate a small part of the image, use this tool to zoom in on a specific area to make it easier to work on.

HAND If the image is too large to fit on your computer screen, use this tool to move the image within its window.

CATALOGUING SOFTWARE

Once you start using cataloguing software to organize how your images are stored on the computer, you will soon appreciate how useful it is. Gone are the days when you spend hours looking for a picture because you can't remember where you stored it on the hard disk. These very useful packages arrange your photographs into an electronic photo album, providing a number of thumbnails on the screen, which you can scroll through to find the right picture.

You can usually add some information for future reference. If you have lots of pictures of your children, say, you can type their name in the information box for each picture. Then, when you want to view a picture of them again, all you need do is type their name in and the software will produce a screen full of thumbnails of the relevant pictures.

OTHER SOFTWARE

Plug-ins are software programs designed to work with established programs. For instance, there are several plug-ins available for Adobe Photoshop, the industry standard in image manipulation software. These plug-ins add a few additional features to your software and offer a relatively inexpensive way of upgrading your existing software. They are often supplied free of charge on CD-ROMs in magazines.

CDs containing royalty-free images are an excellent way of practising your digital imaging skills. These CD-ROMs are packed full of high quality images that you are free to use without paying any royalties. *The National Geographic*, for example, which has established itself over the years as a source of some of the most breathtaking photographs of the world around us, produces a CD-ROM containing 3,000 images that can be used to spice up your own pictures.

Labelling software is available for creating your own customized labels for various items including slide mounts, floppy disks and CDs. These are usually inexpensive and very easy to use. ∎

The pick of the best software

Adobe PhotoDeluxe 3.0 (PC ONLY)
Beginners to image manipulation are well advised to try this software package. It is designed for beginners and is very easy to use. It is packed with plenty of features including comprehensive retouching facilities and special effects.

Photo Recall Deluxe 2.0 (PC ONLY)
This excellent cataloguing software package is very user-friendly and offers comprehensive database utilities. As well as creating photo albums, you can publish pictures on the Internet or e-mail them to your friends and relatives. You can even attach sound to your pictures.

MGI PhotoSuite II (PC ONLY)
A comprehensive package that features almost everything you could possibly need. As well as image manipulation, PhotoSuite offers a database facility, electronic slide show and access to Internet services. Other plus points are its relatively low price and ease of use.

Kai's Photo Soap (PC/MAC)
Image manipulation software doesn't come much more user-friendly than this. The package might lack some of the features of other programs but it makes up for this with its ease of use and low price.

Digital darkroom

Up until recently, if you wanted to process your own photographs at home, the only way you could do so was to invest in expensive and bulky darkroom equipment, which meant handling toxic chemicals in complete darkness.

Today, however, home computers offer a cleaner, faster and more convenient way of producing images. With the right software package you can also manipulate your photographs to create weird and wonderful effects.

Playing around with your images on screen is relatively easy and can be great fun. Not only can you achieve dazzling special effects that would be impossible in a conventional darkroom, but you can also use the software to correct any imperfections on your photographs. This includes such things as removing red eye, retouching, cropping, eliminating scratches and dust from damaged photographs, and correcting colour casts.

The digital darkroom – your home computer – offers enormous scope for producing innovative pictures. The only limit is your own imagination. ∎

Cleaning and removing red eye

Often an image can be spoiled by red eye, caused by the flash reflecting off the back of the eye. Fortunately it's easy enough to correct the problem and clean up the pictures at the same time.

⋂ Red eye is noticeable in the original and the print also shows plenty of dust.

⋂ Using the Remove Dust/Scratch tool and the Remove Red Eye tool has improved the image.

Sepia toning

Certain pictures look better when they appear as if they were taken many years ago. Adding an old-fashioned sepia tone to images is easy to achieve with most types of software.

C This sailing boat made an ideal subject for sepia toning. The first step is to convert the image to black and white.

➲ A muddy brown colour tint was then selected and blur was added to exaggerate the aged effect. The softer look of the picture combines with the colour to produce an old-fashioned effect.

Fun effects

You're wondering what you can do with your pictures to make them look more unusual and exciting? Most software packages offer an enormous number of special effects, so have fun experimenting.

ᴓ Selecting a paint brush effect transforms this picture into a painting.

ᴓ This picture has been manipulated to look as though it has been folded at the corner.

Troubleshooting

Sooner or later you will have a set of photographs returned only to discover that some or all of them haven't turned out as well as you would have expected. What went wrong? This section looks at the most common problems and how you can avoid them.

BLANK FILM

An entirely blank film is a sign that it has not received any exposure. A slide film will be completely black, while a negative will be transparent. The most common reason for this is that the film has not wound onto frame one when loaded. Every time you load a film, check the frame counter to see if '1' is showing. Most compacts display an 'E' for 'Error' if the film has not been loaded correctly.

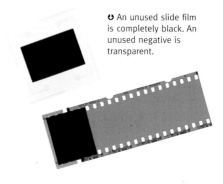

↻ An unused slide film is completely black. An unused negative is transparent.

↻ This holiday photograph has been ruined by camera shake due to the flash not firing.

CAMERA SHAKE

This occurs when the shutter speed is too slow for hand-held shots, resulting in a blurred image. It is most common when the light level is low and the flash has been turned off. One way of avoiding camera shake is to switch the flash on. If this isn't possible then mount the camera on a tripod or use a faster speed film.

➲ Bright, wiggly highlights are another indication of camera shake. In this instance a brilliant purple sunset has been spoiled because the camera was not kept steady.

DOUBLE EXPOSURE

This occurs when the same film has been put through a camera twice, resulting in one set of images being superimposed onto another. It is a double blow because it means that two sets of pictures have been lost.

With 35mm films, make sure the leader is completely rewound into the cassette when you take the film out and write on the film cassette when you remove the film so that you know it has been used.

↻ Processing a film as soon as it is finished will ensure that you don't use the same film twice, as has happened here.

BLEACHED FLASH SHOT

There are two potential reasons for this problem. The first is that the subject is too close and the flash has been too powerful. Check the camera's instructions to determine the minimum distance for flash photography. The second explanation is that the photograph hasn't been printed correctly. Have a reprint made and ask the processor to expose for the subject's face.

↻ These subjects were far too close to the camera, resulting in their faces being overexposed.

SCRATCH ACROSS THE FRAME

This could be due to a grain of grit or sand in the film transport system. Or it could be that the processing machine is scratching your film. If the problem recurs, try a different processor and if it is still present have the camera cleaned.

↻ A scratch has marred an otherwise stunning shot of Paris at night.

OUT-OF-FOCUS SHOTS

This usually occurs because the subject is too close, or the autofocus system has failed to lock onto the subject. Prevent this by making sure your subject is not too close and is covered by the AF sensor. Use the green lamp in the viewfinder as confirmation that the AF system has successfully focused on the subject.

 Here the camera has focused in front of the subject, with the result that neither the subject nor the background is sharp. This problem is usually the fault of the photographer, rather than the camera.

FLARE

Flare often occurs when you are taking a picture with a bright light source included in, or just outside, the frame. Flare, appearing as coloured dots or bright specks, is the result of stray light reaching the lens.

The easiest way to avoid flare from the sun is to take the picture with the sun behind you. Alternatively, wait until a cloud passes in front of the sun. Shielding the lens from the light with your hand also helps to reduce flare.

↩ Shoot into the sun and it's likely that your picture will suffer from flare. Shield the lens with your hand or shoot with the sun behind you.

VERY DARK SUBJECT

This occurs when the photograph has been underexposed, usually because the scene is brighter than normal. Use the camera's spot facility if available and meter from a grey part of the scene. Or use the backlighting compensation (BLC) or exposure compensation facility.

↪ The bright sky in the background has led to the camera underexposing the subject. Using fill-in flash or BLC would have produced a better result.

DARK IMAGES WITH FLASH

The range of a compact's integral flash is limited to a few metres. If your subject is outside this range then it is likely that the picture will appear extremely dark. One way around this problem is to move closer to your subject. You could also try using a faster speed film as this increases the range of the flash.

↺ When distant subjects appear dark, get closer or use a faster film.

FOGGING

Open the camera back while a film is loaded and you will allow stray light into the camera, fogging any exposed film. The extent of the fogging depends on the amount of light getting into the camera. Fogged images appear with large bleached white or red areas. To avoid this, always handle the camera with care. ∎

↺ Accidentally opening the camera for a split second fogged part of the frame. If the camera back had been left open, this frame, along with several others, would have been ruined.

Self-test

Test your knowledge of compact and digital photography with these multiple-choice questions. They vary in difficulty and cover all the subjects we've looked at in the book. So grab a pen and paper – you may be surprised at how much you know.

Check the answers at the end to see how well you've scored:

BELOW 25: Keep learning and practising.
25–40: You've learned a good deal but there's room for improvement.
OVER 40: Excellent knowledge. Practise your photography and gain more experience with the technique projects in Chapter 2.

1. What does APS stand for?
a. Advanced Picture System
b. Advanced Photo System
c. Advanced Photo Software

2. What are SmartMedia and CompactFlash types of?
a. Flash systems
b. Storage cards for digital cameras
c. Autofocus systems

3. What is the term given to the phenomenon of buildings appearing to be leaning backward in photographs?
a. Converging verticals
b. Panoramics
c. Perspective compression

4. What causes red eye?
a. The wrong type of film
b. Bright artificial lighting
c. The reflection of flash from the retina

5. The tolerance of film to over- or underexposure is known as?
a. Exposure latitude
b. Exposure compensation
c. DX-coding

6. Which of the following is the widest aperture?
a. f/3.5
b. f/8
c. f/11

7. What does ISO stand for?
a. International Standards Organisation
b. Internal Software Organisation
c. Identification Systems Organisation

8. What colour is the DX-code chequerboard on a 35mm film cassette?
a. Red and black
b. Silver and black
c. White and black

9. Parallax error causes problems in which photographic technique?
a. Night photography
b. Architectural photography
c. Close-up photography

10. What is 'pixel' short for?
a. Picture extreme
b. Picture element
c. Picture elevation

11. What is the major principle of composition?
a. The rule of halves
b. The rule of thirds
c. The rule of quarters

12. What is the Bulb mode used for?
a. Photographing flowers
b. Taking pictures with flash
c. Long exposures

13. Which of the following is a wide-angle lens?
a. 28mm
b. 90mm
c. 150mm

14. What is the maximum number of exposures on an APS film?
a. 15
b. 30
c. 40

15. What is a 'flatbed' a type of?
a. Printer
b. Scanner
c. Computer

16. Which APS print format is most suitable for landscapes?
a. Classic
b. HDTV
c. Panoramic

17. Which feature is useful for taking pictures through glass?
a. Spot mode
b. Infinity mode
c. Self timer

18. Which of the following cause problems for autofocus systems?
a. Highly reflective surfaces
b. Shooting through bars
c. Both of the above

19. Which type of film is most suitable for hand-held, low-light photography?
a. Slow-speed film
b. Medium-speed film
c. Fast-speed film

20. What is a 'Zip' or a 'JAZ'?
a. External storage
b. An inkjet printer
c. A scanner

21. Taking two or more exposures on the same frame is known as?
a. Overexposure
b. Continuous shooting
c. Multiple exposure

22. What is useful when photographing sunsets?
a. A black-and-white film
b. Spot metering
c. A lightbox

23. What is 'fill-in' an example of?
a. A focusing system
b. A software program
c. Flash mode

24. What are 'magic wands' and 'rubber stamps'?
a. Software programs
b. Autofocus systems
c. Image manipulation tools

25. Which of the following should you use when shooting fireworks?
a. Slow shutter speed
b. Infrared film
c. Red-eye reduction

26. What type of lens produces perspective compression?
a. Wide-angle
b. Telephoto
c. Both types

27. What does IX stand for?
a. Information Exchange
b. Intelligent Crossover
c. Intelligence Exchange

28. What is the technique used for focusing on an off-centre subject?
a. Central locking
b. Exposure compensation
c. Focus lock

29. What does SCSI stand for?
a. Standard Computer Scanner Interface
b. Small Computer Systems Interface
c. Selective Conference Software Interface

30. What are C-41 and E-6 examples of?
a. Slow speed films
b. Types of film processing
c. Battery sizes

31. Which of the following apertures produces the most depth-of-field?
a. f/4
b. f/8
c. f/11

32. What is the speed of a computer's processor measured in?
a. Mb
b. MHz
c. Mph

33. What is the name for devices such as scanners and printers?
a. SmartMedia
b. Software
c. Peripherals

34. What causes a subject to appear too dark in a photograph?
a. Overexposure
b. Underexposure
c. Poor focusing

35. What does CCD stand for?
a. Computer Chip Device
b. Charged Coupled Device
c. Colour Copier Device

36. What type of people picture involves the subject not knowing they are being photographed?
a. Environmental portrait
b. Spy portrait
c. Candid portrait

37. What are centre-weighted and multi-zone types of?
a. Focusing systems
b. Computer systems
c. Metering systems

38. What connects a computer and telephone line?
a. A CD-ROM
b. A scanner
c. A modem

39. Which of the following lenses is the ideal choice for portraits?
a. 28mm
b. 35mm
c. 90mm

40. What should you not use when photographing a floodlit building?
a. A tripod
b. Slow shutter speed
c. Flash

41. What are Kodak Gold and Fuji Superia examples of?
a. Colour slide film
b. Colour print film
c. Black-and-white film

42. What is the resolution of a printer measured in?
a. dpi
b. ppm
c. pixels

43. How should you photograph stained-glass windows?
a. Shoot from the outside
b. Shoot from inside
c. Use the flash

44. What are the Canon IXUS and Pentax efina examples of?
a. Digital cameras
b. APS zoom compacts
c. 35mm compacts

45. How do you remove shadows from a subject's eyes?
a. Have the subject wear a hat
b. Use fill-in flash
c. Switch the flash off

46. What feature on a digital camera allows you to view pictures stored in its memory?
a. The optical viewfinder
b. The self timer
c. The LCD monitor

47. What is the effect caused by stray light entering the camera?
a. Overexposure
b. Flare
c. Red eye

48. What does the '1' on an APS film cartridge indicate?
a. The film has not been used
b. The film has been partly used
c. The film has been processed

49. Which of the following is the most powerful zoom currently on a 35mm compact?
a. 38–115mm
b 48–200mm
c 28–300mm

50. What is the best way to learn photography?
a. Take lessons at school
b. Take evening classes
c. Through experience and practice

The answers: 1:b; 2:b; 3:a; 4:c; 5:a; 6:a; 7:a; 8:b; 9:c; 10:b; 11:b; 12:c; 13:a; 14:c; 15:a; 16:c; 17:b; 18:c; 19:c; 20:a; 21:c; 22:b; 23:c; 24:c; 25:a; 26:b; 27:a; 28:c; 29:b; 30:a; 31:c; 32:b; 33:c; 34:b; 35:b; 36:c; 37:c; 38:c; 39:c; 40:c; 41:b; 42:a; 43:b; 44:b; 45:b; 46:c; 47:b; 48:a; 49:b; 50:c.

Glossary

Aperture
The 'hole' in the lens through which the light passes to reach the film. The size of the aperture is displayed as an f/number. The higher the f/number, the smaller the aperture. Each step from one aperture value to the next is described as a stop. The sequence is as follows (from wide to narrow): f/1, f/1.4, f/2, f/2.8, f/4, f/5.6, f/8, f/11, f/16, f/22, f/32.

Autoexposure
Sensors in the camera measure the amount of light and automatically determine the correct exposure.

Autofocus
Press the shutter button halfway and the camera measures how far away the subject is and automatically adjusts the lens to produce a sharp image. There are two main types of autofocus. Active systems use an infrared beam which measures the subject distance, whereas passive systems have sensors which detect the contrast of the subject to determine the focus.

Most cameras feature a single autofocus point in the centre of the frame, although more advanced cameras have three or more AF sensors spread across the frame.

Backlighting compensation (BLC)
This is used when you take a picture where the subject has a bright background and it's likely that it will appear too dark. Using backlighting compensation adds some exposure and increases the odds that the subject will appear correctly exposed.

Bit
Short for binary digit, this is the smallest form of information in a computer. Eight bits equals one byte. The more bits in a pixel, the better the resolution and colour.

Bracketing
This involves taking a series of pictures at slightly different exposure settings to obtain one picture at the correct exposure. Some cameras have an autoexposure bracketing feature which takes a series of three shots.

Byte
A unit of computer memory or storage. Each byte comprises eight bits. One kilobyte (Kb) is 1024 bytes, one megabyte (Mb) is 1024 kilobytes and one gigabyte (Gb) is 1024 megabytes.

Bulb
An exposure mode that keeps the shutter open for as long as you keep the shutter button depressed. Useful for taking creative night shots.

C-41 process
The standard process for developing colour negative films.

CCD
A charge-coupled device is an electronic sensor that converts light into an electronic signal to form a digital image.

CD-ROM
Compact Disk-Read Only Memory. Each disk can hold up to a maximum of 650Mb of information in the form of text, sound or digital images.

CD-ROM drive
A device which 'reads' the CD-ROM. Now a standard feature on almost all home computers; available as an optional accessory for older models.

Chromogenic film
A film which forms the final image from dyes rather than silver. Some black-and-white films use chromogenic technology.

Coatings
A transparent layer applied to the lens optics to protect it from damage and also to improve optical quality by reducing reflections and improving contrast.

Colour cast
This is the result of poor printing or shooting daylight balanced film under artificial light.

Compression
Digital images take up a lot of memory so compression is used to keep down the size of the file. This means more images can be stored and that they can be transmitted quicker. Some image detail is lost, so the higher the compression, the more noticeable the loss.

CPU
The Central Processing Unit determines how fast a computer can handle information. For digital imaging, a Pentium 133MHz (or equivalent) is the minimum you should use.

Cropping
Cropping involves trimming away parts of an image to improve its composition.

Cross processing
This technique involves processing a colour film in the wrong chemistry to produce bizarre effects. For instance, processing a colour print film in E-6 (colour slide process) or a colour slide film in C-41 (colour print film process).

Depth-of-field
The amount of the scene in front and behind the subject that appears sharp. In general, the smaller the aperture, the greater the depth-of-field and vice versa.

Download
Transferring a file from another computer to your own, usually via a modem.

DPI
Dots per inch. A measurement for the resolution of a printer, scanner or computer monitor. The more dots per inch, the higher the resolution.

DVD
Digital Versatile Disk. The latest standard in information storage. A DVD holds 9Gb, around 14 times the amount of data that a CD-ROM can handle.

DX-coding
The pattern of black and silver rectangles on a 35mm film cassette that determines the film speed. DX-coded compacts feature pins that read the pattern and set the film speed automatically.

Dye sublimation
A method of printing that creates photographic-quality results. It uses heat to place colour from a foil onto the paper.

E-6 process
The standard process for colour slide films.

E-mail
An electronic form of mail. Text, sound and images can all be sent by e-mail.

Exposure compensation
A feature found on only a few compacts that allows you to set more or less exposure than that set by the camera.

Exposure latitude
This is the tolerance of a film to over- or underexposure. Print films have a very wide latitude, so they can handle large exposure errors. Slide films have a very narrow latitude and require accurate exposures to produce an acceptable image.

File format
Digital images are stored in one of several file formats. The most popular types are JPEG, TIFF and Photo CD.

Film format
There are two main types of film format for compact cameras: 35mm film is the most popular, but the Advanced Photo System (APS), introduced in 1996, is steadily gaining a larger market share.

Fixed-focus lens
The focus of the lens is non-adjustable and relies on depth-of-field to produce a sharp image.

Flare
Stray light which spoils images by producing patches of light on the photo. Most common when taking pictures while facing the sun.

Flash modes
Most compact cameras have an integral flashgun with various modes. Autoflash fires the flash when required. Forced-on and forced-off modes allow you to override the autoflash. Slow-sync fires the flash and selects a long shutter speed for creative effects.

Floppy disk
A removable storage media for holding text, sound or images. The 3.5in floppy has a maximum storage capacity of 1.44Mb so it can hold only relatively small image files.

Focus lock
Found on most autofocus compacts, this allows you to focus on a subject by pressing the shutter button halfway while the subject is in the centre of the frame. This enables you to recompose, with the button still partially pressed, and keep the main subject in focus.

Focusing steps
An autofocus lens has a certain number of focusing positions relating to the subject distance. These positions are termed focusing steps. The more steps there are, the more accurate the focusing mechanism.

Fogging
Unwanted exposure of the film. This usually occurs when the camera back is opened accidentally.

GIF
This stands for Graphical Interchange Format and is a common file format for images on the Internet.

Gigabyte
A unit of computer memory or storage. A gigabyte is equivalent to 1024 megabytes.

Grain
Groups of silver halides which form the image. The general rule is that the faster the film speed, the larger the grain and the less sharp the image.

Guide number
A standard indication for the power output of a flashgun. The higher the guide number, the more powerful the flash. It is based on an ISO 100 film and stated in metres.

Hard disk
The 'brain' of a computer. The hard disk stores all the programs, images and text files. The larger the hard-disk memory, the more it can store.

Hot spot
The reflection of an integral flashgun off a shiny reflection such as a window.

Image manipulation
Digitally altering an image. This can involve minor changes or the complete transformation of the original image.

Infinity lock
A feature found on autofocus cameras using the active system (infrared beams) to focus on the subject. This type of AF system has trouble focusing through glass so an infinity lock feature is often included on the camera to set the lens to focus on infinity beyond the glass.

Information exchange (IX)
APS film uses a magnetic strip which records exposure information and transfers it to the processing equipment. The most common IX features are Date and Time imprinting, Mid-Roll Change (MRC), Print Format Selection, Print Quality Improvement (PQI), Print Quantity (PQ) and Titling.

Inkjet printer
One of the most common types of printer. It works by spraying tiny dots of ink onto the paper to produce an image.

Interpolation
A software method of increasing the apparent image detail by averaging out the densities of a series of pixels and placing a new pixel in between.

Intervalometer
Used for time-lapse photography. It takes a series of pictures at regular intervals ranging from minutes to hours.

ISO
International Standards Organisation. This is the system for determining the film speed. Replaces the previous ASA and DIN ratings.

JPEG
Joint Photographic Experts Group. A common type of file format for compressed images.

LCD monitor

Some digital cameras feature an LCD monitor which acts as an electronic viewfinder for composing the photograph. Many cameras allow stored images to be reviewed on the monitor, while on some the monitor features an on-screen menu for choosing some of the camera's functions.

LED

Coloured lamps which are often used in the viewfinder to indicate when the autofocus and flash systems are ready. An LED (Light Emitting Diode) is often found on the front of the camera and flashes during a self-timer countdown.

Maximum aperture

The widest setting for the lens iris. The wider the maximum aperture, the easier it is to take decent shots in low light.

Megapixel

This is a term used to describe digital cameras that boast more than one million pixels.

Memory cards

These are removable storage cards that are used to store images. There are several types available, the most common being SmartMedia, CompactFlash and PCMCIA (Personal Computer Memory Card International Association) cards.

Metering patterns

Cameras work out what exposure to set by measuring how much light reflects off the subject. Some cameras offer more than one type of metering pattern.

CENTRE-WEIGHTED AVERAGE: Takes an average reading from the entire frame but gives emphasis to the central part of the frame.
MULTI-ZONE: A system that works by splitting the frame into several zones. The camera uses a complex set of algorithms to work out the exposure.
SPOT: A very precise metering system that takes the exposure reading from a very small area at the centre of the frame.

Modem

MOdulator and DEModulator. A device that connects a computer to the telephone line for access to electronic fax or the Internet.

Morphing

A feature on some image manipulation programs that allows you to distort the appearance of the subject.

Motorwind

Motorized film advance and automatic rewind once the end of the film is reached.

Parallax

The difference in viewpoint between the compact camera's viewfinder and the lens. For most situations the difference causes no problems but with close-ups, parallax correction is needed to compose a picture correctly.

Pixel

The smallest element of a digital image. It carries the colours and resolution that make up the image. The more pixels in an image, the better the quality.

Photo CD
A system developed by Kodak that stores the images on a CD for viewing through dedicated players, a TV or on a computer.

Printer
An inexpensive device for producing a print from your digital image.

RAM
Random Access Memory. The area of the computer's memory where information is temporarily stored. The larger the RAM, the more programs and applications a computer can handle at a time.

Red eye
An annoying problem with flash photography where the pupils of the eyes look red. Many cameras have a red-eye reduction feature for keeping this problem to a minimum.

Resolution
A term to describe the detail and sharpness of an image. With digital images, it can be measured by multiplying the number of vertical and horizontal pixels. The resolution of a printer is often given in dots per inch.

Scanner
A device that converts photos, film or artwork into a digital form. A film scanner scans negatives and slides at high resolution for storage and manipulation on a computer. Most scanners handle 35mm film although many have adaptors to accept APS film. Flatbed scanners are used for scanning prints. Some also scan transparencies.

SCSI
Small Computer Systems Interface. The industry standard interface for connecting peripherals such as scanners.

Self-timer
A facility for delaying the taking of the picture by around ten seconds.

Single-use camera
A cheap fixed-focus compact with a preloaded film that is used only once.

Thumbnail
Smaller versions of a picture. Used on the Index Print of an APS film to show all the photos on a film. Also used on digital software to catalogue and view images.

TIFF
Tagged Image File Format. A popular form of image file format.

Viewfinder
The window in a camera through which you compose the picture. Most have guidelines around the edges and a set of coloured LEDs to show the status of the autofocus and flash.

VRAM
Video Random Access Memory. A graphics card that controls the number of colours that can be seen on screen.

Zoom
A lens with a variable focal length. Some digital cameras feature a 'digital zoom' which works by magnifying the central part of the frame at the cost of some image quality.

Stockists

ActionTec
Johnsons Photopia Ltd,
Hempstalls Lane,
Newcastle,
Staffs ST5 0SW
Tel: 01782 753300
Fax: 01782 753399

Adobe
Waterview House,
1 Roundwood Ave,
Stockley Park,
Uxbridge,
Middlesex UB11 1AY
Tel: 0181 606 4001
Fax: 0181 606 4004

Agfa
27 Great West Road,
Brentford,
Middlesex TW8 9AX
Tel: 0181 560 2131
Fax: 0181 231 4951

Apple Computer (UK) Ltd
2 Furzground Way,
Stockley Park,
Uxbridge,
Middlesex UB11 1BB
Tel: 0181 218 1000
Fax: 0181 569 2957

Canon
Canon House,
Manor Road,
Wallington,
Surrey SM6 OAJ
Tel: 0181 773 6000
Fax: 0181 669 8974

Cobra
5 Capstan Centre,
Thurrock Park Way,
Tilbury,
Essex RM18 7HH
Tel: 01375 840540
Fax: 01375 840534

Contax/Yashica
Unit 7,
Sutton Business Park,
Sutton Park Avenue,
Earley, Reading,
Berks RG6 1AZ
Tel: 0118 935 6300
Fax: 0118 935 6309

Dell
Boghall Road,
Bray, Co Wicklow,
Ireland
Tel: 0500 500111
Fax: 01344 723691

Dixons
Dixons House,
Mayland Avenue,
Hemel Hempstead,
Herts HP2 7TG
Tel: 0541 545560

Epson
Campus 100,
Maylands Ave,
Hemel Hempstead,
Herts HP2 7TJ
Tel: 01442 761212
Fax: 01442 227353

Fuji Photo Film (UK)
Fuji Film House,
125 Finchley Road,
London NW3 6JH
Tel: 0171 586 5900
Fax: 0171 722 4259

Iomega (UK) Ltd
Westacott Way,
Maidenhead,
Berks SL6 3RT
Tel: 01628 822444
Fax: 00353 14105075

Halina
Haking International
Centre,
Welwyn Garden City,
Herts AL7 1L
Tel: 01707 393939
Fax: 01707 390 323

Hanimex/Vivitar
Westmead,
Swindon
Wilts SN5 7XT
Tel: 01793 526211
Fax: 01793 544814

Hewlett-Packard
Cain Road, Bracknell,
Berks RG12 1HN
Tel: 01344 360000
Fax: 01344 363344

Ilford
Town Lane, Mobberley,
Knutsford,
Cheshire WA16 7JL
Tel: 01565 684000
Fax: 01565 873035

Jessop Group
Jessop House,
98 Scudamore Road,
Leicester LE3 1TZ
Tel: 0116 232 0033
Fax: 0116 232 0060

Kodak Limited
Kodak House,
Hemel Hempstead,
Herts HP1 1JU
Tel: 01442 261122
Fax: 01442 240609

Konica (UK) Limited
Plane Tree Crescent,
Feltham, Middx
TW13 7HD
Tel: 0181 751 6121
Fax: 0181 755 0681

Leica Camera Ltd
Davy Avenue,
Milton Keynes
Northants MK5 8LB
Tel: 01908 666663
Fax: 01908 609992

Lexmark
West Thorpe House,
Little Marlow Road,
Marlow,
Bucks SL7 3RQ
Tel: 01628 481500
Fax: 01628 481908

Live Pix
Suite 2, Warstone Court,
Warstone Lane,
Birmingham B18 6JQ
Tel: 0121 236 1990

Microsoft
Freepost GW8554,
Glasgow G3 7BR
Tel: 0345 002000
Fax: 0141 226 4197

Minolta (UK) Ltd
Rooksley Park,
Precedent Drive,
Milton Keynes
Northants MK13 8HF
Tel: 01908 200400
Fax: 01908 200391

Mitsubishi
Travellers Lane,
Hatfield,
Herts AL10 8XB
Tel: 01707 276 100

Nikon
Nikon House,
380 Richmond Road,
Surrey KT2 5PR
Tel: 0181 541 4440
Fax: 0181 541 4584

Olympus
2–8 Honduras Street,
London EC1Y 0TX
Tel: 0171 253 2772
Fax: 0171 490 7880

Pentax (UK) Ltd
Pentax House,
Heron Drive,
Langley, Slough,
Berks SL3 8PN
Tel: 01753 792792
Fax: 01753 792794

Polaroid (UK) Ltd
Wheathampstead House,
Codicote Road,
Wheathampstead,
Herts AL4 8SF
Tel: 01582 632000
Fax: 01582 632001

Ricoh
Hempstalls Lane,
Newcastle,
Staffs ST5 0SW
Tel: 01782 753300
Fax: 01782 753399

Samsung
Samsung House,
3 Riverbank Way,
Great West Road,
Brentford,
Middlesex TW8 9RE
Tel: 0181 862 9311
Fax: 0181 862 0096

Sanyo
Sanyo House,
Otterspool Way,
Watford,
Herts WD2 8JX
Tel: 01923 246363
Fax: 01923 817410

Sony
Pyrene House,
Sunbury Cross,
Sunbury-On-Thames,
Middlesex TW16 7AT
Tel: 0990 111 999
Fax: 01635 875250

Index

A

accessories 72–5, 117
Adobe Photoshop 201
Advanced Photo System *see*
    APS
Agfa 59–63
angle of view 36-7
animals 132–7
Annealed-Polyethylens
    Naphthalate (A-Pen) 24
apertures 52–5, 91, 117,
    212
Apple Macintosh 189, 197
APS (Advanced Photo
    System) 22–7, 66
    advantages 23–4
    black-and-white film 63
    cameras 97, 117
    compact cameras 175
    compacts 186
    films 24–7, 182, 194, 215
    print film 60
    slide films 61
    on TV 27
architecture 127, 138-43
    patterns 170–1
autofocus (AF) 42–7, 64, 66,
    134, 147, 206, 212
    locking 47, 161
automatic mode 20, 170

B

Backlighting Compensation
    (BLC) 18, 207, 212
batteries 19
birds 136–7
bit (binary digit) 212
black-and-white
    documentaries 62, 120–5
    films 57, 62–3, 114, 120–5,
        122, 169
    slide films 63
    tonal range 62
bracketing 212
buildings
    floodlit 150–1, 154–5
    interiors and exteriors 141

bulbs 114, 149, 212
    facility 64, 152, 175–6
    mode 18, 150, 176–6, 183
byte 212, 215

C

C-41
    compatible film 63, 122
    process 180, 212
calendars 71
camera shake 96, 103, 117,
    204
cameras
    buying 64–7
    cases 72
    and equipment 9–75
    outfits 64, 66, 110
    special effects 175–6, 178,
        180, 182
candid shots 100, 106–7
canvas prints 71
care and maintenance 68–9,
    72
cartridges 13, 65, 192
cassettes 23–4, 74
cataloguing software 200–1
CCD (charge-coupled device)
    30, 32, 117, 212
CD-ROMs (Compact Disk
    Read Only) 187, 201, 212
    drives 186, 189, 196, 213
children 100, 108–9
close-ups 16, 112, 116–19
coastlines 97
coatings 213
colours
    cast 213
    contrasting 47, 86–9
    films 57, 87, 149, 175, 214
        infrared 128, 178–9, 183
        medium-speed 176
        slide 61, 149, 161, 180
    filters 178
    temperature 60
    wheel 87
Compact Flash cards 31, 197,
    216

compacts 10–13, 64–6, 117
    film format 22
    multiple exposure facility
        182
    shutter systems 53
    telephoto zoom 103
composition 78–85, 91–4
compression 33, 213
computers
    checklist 187
    compatiblity 67
    hardware 186–9
    ports and slots 187–9
    processing speed 187
    see also floppy disks;
        software
connection sockets 30
countryside 97
CPU (Central Processing
    Unit) 186, 213
cropping 213

D

databack 19
Date and Time imprinting
    215
depth-of-field 54, 117,
    213
digital
    darkrooms 202–3
    imaging 185–201
    lenses 28
    versatile disk (DVD) 213
digital cameras 28–35, 66–7,
    117, 125
    shutter systems 53
dioptric adjustment 17
disc system 13
dot matrix printers 190
download 213
DPI (Dots per inch) 213
DVD (Digital Versatile Disk)
    213
DX-coding 16, 74–5, 178,
    213
dye-sublimation printers
    190, 213

E
E-6 process 63, 180, 214
e-mail 214
environmental portraits 100,
104–5
everyday life 125
exposures 48–55, 133–4, 136
autoexposures 212
calculating 48–9
colours 87
compensation 180, 214
double 205
latitude 58, 122, 125, 182,
214
modes 16
multiple 18, 182–3, 213
special effects 175–6, 178,
182
underexposing 128
exteriors 89, 103, 141
patterns 171
external storage 196–7

F
file format 33, 214, 216–17
films 56–63, 113–14
black-and white 57, 62–3,
65, 120–5, 122, 169
blank 204
chromogenic 63, 213
colour negative 59
colour print 59, 117, 180
colour-slide 61, 161, 180
cross processing 180–1,
183, 213
formats 22, 65
processing 70, 125
retrievers 74
special effects 175, 180, 182
speed override 180
speeds 52, 56–60, 117, 133,
146, 178
filters 74–5, 178
finance schemes 67
fireworks 148–9, 154
fixed
lenses 39, 64

compacts 10, 57, 64
focus 42, 64, 66, 214
wide-angle 66
flare 91, 206, 214
flash 112–3, 205–6
autoflash 161
fill-in 20, 64
flash-off override 42
integral 20–1, 30, 64, 114,
117
modes 214
sensor and light sensor
14
floodlighting 150–1, 154–5
floppy disks 31, 189, 214
flowers and fungi 119
focal
length, comparisons 26,
36–8, 54
points and colour 85
focus 30, 51, 206, 214
fixed lenses 42, 64, 66,
214
lock 47, 141, 161, 214
systems 42–7
see also autofocus (AF)
fogging 206, 214
forced-off mode 20
frame lines/parallax correction
lines 17
Fuji 59–61, 63
fun effects 203
funfairs 152–5

G
GIF (Graphical Interchange
Format) 215
gigabyte 215
glass
shooting through 47
stained-glass windows
144-7
glossary 212–17
grain 215
graphics cards 189
guarantees 67
guide numbers 215

H
half-frame cameras 13
hard
disks 215
drive 187–8
HDTV format 61
high-resolution
cameras 34–5
single-lens reflex (SLR)
35
holding your camera 69
homes 142
hot spots 215

I
Ilford 62
images
compression 33, 213
formats 33
manipulation 215
software 199–200
resolution 32
storage 66
infinity
locks 91, 134, 215
mode 16
Information Exchange (IX)
23, 215
infrared
colour film 128
remote control 153
transceivers 14, 16
inkjet printers 190–1, 197,
215
insects 119
instant cameras 13
interior shots 89, 103, 141–3,
170
internal memory 31
interpolation 32, 215
intervalometers 215
Iomega
JAZ removable hard disks
196
Zip removable hard disks
196
ISO (International Standards

Organisation)
films 56–8, 103, 125,
133–4, 149, 152, 180,
215
speeds 57–8, 117, 133
speed override 180

J, K
JPEG (Joint Photographic
Experts Group) 33, 214–15
Kodak 59–61, 63, 217
Konica 60

L
labelling software 26, 201,
215
landmarks 141
landscapes 16, 62, 90–9,
127
laser printers 190
LCD (Liquid Crystal Display)
monitors 16–17, 30, 67,
117, 216
LEDs (Light Emitting Diode)
17, 216–17
lenses 14, 36–41
cleaning cloths 72
digital cameras 28
focal length comparisons
26, 36–8, 54
see also fixed, telephoto,
wide-angle and zoom
lenses
light and lighting 47, 91, 110,
113, 122, 142
Backlighting
Compensation (BLC) 18,
207, 212
LED (Light Emitting
Diode) 17, 216
see also flash; floodlighting
lightboxes and lupes 75
loading
35mm compacts 17
drop-in 23
low-resolution cameras 34
LZW compression 33

M
macro mode 18
mail order
camera purchases 67
processing 70
mains sockets 30
major events 125
manual focus 46
override 134
maximum aperture 216
medium-resolution cameras
34
megapixel 216
cameras 34–5, 66
memory cards 31, 197,
216
metering 141, 161, 216
centre-weighted 49
and focusing sensors 30
multi-zone 49, 51
spot 49–51, 158
systems 48–52
mid-roll change (MRC) 23–4,
215
Minox spy cameras 13
MMX (MultiMedia
eXtensions) 186
mode dials 30
modems (MOdulator-
DEModulators) 196,
216
monitors 186–7
see also LCD (Liquid Crystal
Display)
morphing 216
motorwinds 16-17, 216
moving subjects 47, 53-4

N, O
National Geographic 201
negatives 24, 59, 194
neon signs 89
night scenes 148–55
novelty compacts 13
one-hour processing 70
optical viewfinders 30
out-of-focus shots 206

P
panoramic facility 18
parallax 119, 216
patterns 168–73
PCMCIA (Personal Computer
Memory Card International
Association) cards 31,
197, 216
PCs (IBM compatible) 189,
197
Pentium processors 186
people 100–9
peripherals 190–7
pets 132, 136–7
Filters 74
photo CD (file format) 214,
216
photo CD-ROMs 71
photos, using 71
pixel 216
portraiture 16, 100, 102–3
presentation 75
printers 190–3, 216
printing
costs 191
paper 193
speeds 191
prints
formats 24, 26
selection 215
quality improvement (PQI)
26, 215
quantity (PQ) 26
size 191
processors 186

R
RAM (Random Access
Memory) 187–8, 216
Random Access Memory see
RAM; VRAM
rangefinders 11–12
red eye 217
cleaning and removing 202
reduction 20, 64, 133
reflective surfaces 47, 113,
128, 147, 150

reflectors 74, 117
remote control 17
reprints 70
resolution 197, 217
cameras 32, 34–5
rewritable CD-ROM drive
196
rule of thirds 78–85, 91,
120

S
scanners 194–5, 217
flatbed 194–5
software 194–5
speeds 195
scratches across the frame
205
screen displays 198–9
SCSI (Small Computer
Systems Interface) 197, 217
self-tests 208–11
self-timers 217
35mm compacts 16
lamps 30
sepia toning 203
servo AF 45–6
shareware 199
shooting 18, 47, 64
shutters
speeds 19, 53–5, 150, 175,
212
systems 53
silhouettes 164–7
silica gel 72
single-lens reflex (SLR)
cameras 35
single-use cameras 12, 217
slide
accessories 75
films 61, 63, 65, 70, 75,
175, 204
colour 61, 149, 161, 180
slow-synchronization mode
19–20
SmartMedia cards (memory
cards) 31, 197, 216
sockets 30

software 198–201
packages 189
printers 192
scanners 194–5
special effects 174–83, 203
spot
AF 45
facilities 164
metering 49–51, 64, 158
status indicators 23
still life 110–15, 119
stockists 67, 218
storage
card readers 197
external 196–7
images 66
negatives within cassettes
24
subjects 47, 206
exposure modes 16
movement 47, 53–4
to-camera distance 55
sunsets 156–63
SVGA (Super VGA cameras)
34
System Developing
Companies (SDC) 22

T
T-Max developers 63
T-shirts and jigsaws 71
techniques 77–183
telephoto lenses 37, 96–7,
103, 142
zoom 96, 103, 134, 139–40
35mm
compacts 14–21, 65–6, 175,
186
Backlighting
Compensation (BLC) 18,
207, 212
films 205
black-and-white 62–3,
65
print 59–60, 65
slide 61, 65
negatives 194

three or four-hour processing
70
thumbnails 217
TIFF (Tagged Image File
Format) 33, 214, 217
titling 26, 215
traffic trails 174–5, 183
travel 126–31
tripods 73, 96, 149, 155
troubleshooting 204–7
TTL (Through The Lens)
systems 30
tungsten lighting 113
TWAIN (Technology Without
An Interesting Name) 195
24-hour processing 70
twin LEDs 17

U, V
underwater housing 74
VGA (Video Graphics Array)
cameras 34
viewfinders 17, 30, 217
viewpoints 94–7, 139
VRAM (Video Random
Access Memory) 189, 217

W
warranties 67
waterproof cameras 12–13
weather-resistant cameras
12–13, 64
wide-angle lenses 36–7, 66,
96, 140, 149–50, 152, 175
uses 122, 128, 141–2, 145

X, Z
XGA (Extended GA cameras)
34
zoo animals 134–5, 137
zoom
compacts 10–11, 64, 122,
125, 133, 142, 158, 175
control 30
lenses 39, 58, 66, 96, 103,
125, 128, 139–40, 145,
169, 217

Acknowledgments

All photography by **Daniel Lezano** except for the following pages: 25 (top) and 129 (top) **Iain Bagwell**; 21 and 121 (top) **Sandra Doble**; 107, 109, 128, 134 and 166 **Phil Gamble**; 108 **Dave Goodman**; 184–185 **Euan Myles/Tony Stone Images**; 122 and 151 **Ralph Pitchford** 2, 46, 92–93, 97, 98–99, 103 (left), 106 (left), 110–111, 116, 118, 126, 130–131 and 133 **John Sootheran**; 121(bottom), 123 and 158 **Omri Stephenson**.

Special Photography: pages 4–5, 6–7, 8–9, 22–23, 58–63, 193 and 208–210 **Iain Bagwell**; pages 1, 3, 10–11, 12, 14–15, 26, 28–29, 31, 34–35, 37, 65, 69, 71, 72–73, 186–187, 188, 190–191, 192, 194–195, 196–197 and 204, **Andrew Sydenham**.

Illustrations: pages 37, 87, **Phil Gamble**

The publisher would like to thank the following organizations for generously allowing us to photograph their cameras: **Dixons, Fuji, Kodak, Olympus** and **Pentax**.

A special thank you to the following people for their help: **Charlie Allen, Patrick Carpenter, Dan Green, Tom Ruppel** and **Iain Wright**.

The author would also like to thank **John Sootheran** (Max Power), **Peter Bargh** (Digital PhotoFX), **William Cheung** (Practical Photography), **Clare Fleerackers** (Kodak), **Hewlett Packard** and **Madaline Miller** (Emap).